Sharing Mindsets

Sharing Mindsets

Where Classrooms and Businesses Meet

Joy Rosser and Anthony Barber

ROWMAN & LITTLEFIELD
Lanham • Boulder • New York • London

Published by Rowman & Littlefield
An imprint of The Rowman & Littlefield Publishing Group, Inc.
4501 Forbes Boulevard, Suite 200, Lanham, Maryland 20706
www.rowman.com

6 Tinworth Street, London SE11 5AL, United Kingdom

Copyright © 2020 by Joy Rosser and Anthony Barber

All rights reserved. No part of this book may be reproduced in any form or by any electronic or mechanical means, including information storage and retrieval systems, without written permission from the publisher, except by a reviewer who may quote passages in a review.

British Library Cataloguing in Publication Information Available

Library of Congress Cataloging-in-Publication Data Available

ISBN: 978-1-4758-4061-2 (cloth)
ISBN: 978-1-4758-4062-9 (pbk.)
ISBN: 978-1-4758-4063-6 (electronic)

Contents

Foreword ... ix
Ron Jaworski, former quarterback, Philadelphia Eagles;
CEO, Ron Jaworski Golf; co-owner, Philadelphia Soul

Preface ... xi

Acknowledgments ... xiii

Introduction ... xv

Part I: An Inward Journey of the Self ... 1

1 Just a Rough Launch, Not Going to Be a Bad Day!
 Gain Momentum from Moments ... 3
 Douglas C. Yearley Jr., chairman and CEO, Toll Brothers

2 What D'ya Mean I Can't Redo the Day?
 Honor Life's Brevity ... 7
 H. Edward Hanway, former CEO, Cigna Corporation

3 Become the Family Dog!
 Personalize Your Behaviors ... 11
 Ed Herr, president and CEO, Herr Foods, Inc.

4 At What Cost? And We Don't Mean Money!
 Embrace Your Boundaries ... 15
 Rakia Reynolds, founder and CEO, Skai Blue Media

5 Call Your Own Timeout in Your Life Game!
   Assess and Recalibrate   19
   Gary Jonas Jr., president, The HOW Group

6 Be the Giving Tree, but First Water Your Roots!
   Be Selfish to Be Generous   23
   Andrea Gilbert, president, Bryn Mawr Hospital

7 Life's Not Meeting You Halfway, Go Out and Get It!
   Let Your Attitude Be the Catalyst   27
   *Pete Ciarrocchi, chairman and CEO, Chickie's & Pete's Crab
   House and Sports Bar*

Part II: An Outward Journey of the Heart   31

8 Put in a Contributing Piece to Someone Else's Puzzle
   Trust the Process   33
   Angelo R. Perryman, president and CEO, Perryman Construction

9 Put on Your Glasses and Really SEE the Person!
   Cultivate Strengths   37
   Marcus Allen, CEO, Big Brothers Big Sisters Independence Region

10 Seeing Problems? You Might Need New Glasses!
   View Challenges as Opportunities   43
   *Bernard Dagenais, president and CEO, The Main Line
   Chamber of Commerce*

11 Engaging with People Can Actually Be Fun? Yes It Can!
   Invest in Relationships   47
   Chris Gheysens, president and CEO, Wawa, Inc.

12 Labels Are Just for Soup Cans
   Define Hearts, Despite Actions   53
   *Denis P. O'Brien, senior executive VP,
   advisor to CEO, Exelon Corporation*

13 Silence Is Golden—Perfect for the Theater, Not for Life!
   Recognize the Power of Response   57
   *William J. Marrazzo, president and
   CEO, WHYY, Inc.*

14 What Floor Is Your Mood Elevator On?
   Inspire through Illuminating   63
   Thomas Mehler, president, Southco, Inc.

Part III: An Impactful Journey of the Hands — 69

15 Just Napkins? Come On, You Can Do Better Than That! Support and Serve — 71
Nicholas J. Giuffre, former president and CEO, Bradford White Corporation

16 But I Really Thought People Liked Hearing Me Complain! Reflect and Accept — 77
Kevin Reilly, former NFL player, motivational speaker, and author

17 Passing the Mashed Potatoes and Saying "Thank You," It Really Is That Simple! Appreciate and Encourage — 81
Phil Martelli, former head men's basketball coach, St. Joseph's University

18 Large Coffee, Extra Passion, and Two Heaping Spoonfuls of Creativity! Experience and Navigate — 87
Nick Bayer, CEO and founder, Saxbys

19 We're Talking about Connections, Man! I Mean How Silly Is That? We're Talking about Connections! Connect and Cultivate — 93
Chris Franklin, chairman and CEO, Aqua America with Nick DeBenedictis, former chairman and CEO; current board member, Aqua America

20 What If You Were Paid to Sell the Greatness of Your Workplace? Would You Be a Millionaire? Brand and Promote — 99
John Leahy, former president and COO, KIND Healthy Snacks

21 Examine Your Enthusiasm for Life, Hope You Don't Need a Microscope! Ignite Hearts — 103
Andrew Stine, teacher, Twin Valley Middle School

About the Editors — 107

About the Contributors — 109

Foreword

I have always believed that the key to success stems from one's ability to set lofty goals and work hard to attain them. Be it on the football field or in the business arena, the difference between success and failure can come down to inches, and the desire to prosper can be realized or vanished in an instant. Therefore, it is only with passion and purpose that we make our own opportunities to be highly successful.

Throughout the years, I have noticed that there are various similarities between being an NFL quarterback and also a CEO or leader of a company. Despite the differences in each job task, underlying principles (like the ones mentioned earlier) guide my work each day. And although no one is trying to literally sack me in the board room, competitors exist who would not mind if Jaws hit the carpet one more time.

My friends Joy and Tony, both of whom are educators, have a similar thought process when it comes to their profession and the business world. Like the learning I have experienced, they also believe that crossover skills exist that assist both educators and business leaders.

When they approached me about this book, I thought this endeavor was much needed. Being able to chat with some of my successful colleagues in the business world and use their achievements to assist educators just makes sense. Although I had never heard of a book that combined the successful traits of CEOs and educators, I was fascinated by the prospect of not only assisting educators, but, ultimately, our students.

Sharing Mindsets: Where Classrooms and Businesses Meet is a candid book that devotes itself to practical topics, using relatable stories and anecdotes to illustrate critical points. Within these stories, Joy and Tony offer hands-on suggestions to help the reader find resolutions to common issues facing leadership moments. Both Joy and Tony bring their years of educational experiences to the text; combine that with twenty-three of the most admired CEOs and leaders in America right now, and you have a can't-miss book that any educator and business person can appreciate.

In closing, there are those that say that education is a people business. In my world, any business is a people business, and I invite you to read, think, and improve your ability to be a great, teacher, educator, business person, and leader by embracing the many skills discussed in this tremendous book.

—Ron Jaworski

Preface

We are so often asked, "What is the role of a teacher?"

A teacher's purpose is to enlighten young minds; to monitor student interactions; to teach a wide array of curricula and skills; to assist parents; to prepare our youth for the next grade, the next level, the next journey; to evaluate achievement and effort; to care deeply enough that it creates care in others; to influence and lead such that the followers become independent thinkers and leaders themselves. The list is infinite and could be a book in and of itself.

However, we are often retorted by others who say that the "real-world" exists outside of the classroom. In this "real" realm, the bottom line is production and, well, the bottom line. Often times, this world is presented as a much harder place, one where growth can only be attained on someone else's time. A place where the only thing that matters is the company's success.

Although positioned as the powerful negative of society, there must exist some silver lining in this counter-world. In other words, are schools and businesses that far off? Are we simply preparing students for a place that does not exist? Or perhaps is business being painted in a dark light by those who may not know its light, quality side?

As educators, we thought about these questions, we assumed there had to be some type of middle ground between education and business. Truth be told, since a third grader does not know that she wants to be a sales representative for KIND, and since an eighth grader does not know that he wants to be a manager at his local Chickie's & Pete's, and since a high school senior does not know that he wants to sell water heaters for Bradford White Corporation, do we not have the responsibility to bridge the gap with the expected and anticipated *values* of companies and ourselves? In this sense, we must teach and wear our classroom values as they pertain to the greater, larger picture for students who ultimately become employees.

Starting on the turf we know best, the classroom, we identified messages that we have seen create the best teacher from a *self*-perspective, a *relational* perspective, and an *extension* perspective. In other words, how teachers can be best for themselves, for those around them, and for the community.

Then we sought out Philadelphia and Greater Philadelphia leaders and CEOs to support their values and provide the why. Why does it matter that teachers invest relationally in students? Why does it matter that teachers put themselves first so they can be generous for others? Why does it matter that teachers love unconditionally?

This text demonstrates that the educational and corporate messages are the same and that what we expect of ourselves as educators and from students is what is expected at the corporate level (no matter how close to, or far from, the top of that corporation someone's role might be). The book aims at getting everyone to feel supported and connected because too often we operate in separate bubbles.

As teachers, we need to invest relationally like Wawa invests in its associates and customers because it creates a unique culture where people *want* to be. We need to put ourselves first because nurses at Bryn Mawr Hospital do the same for the benefit of their patients. We need to create a climate where loving unconditionally matters because Herr's is successfully doing that every day in its community and within its boardroom.

Broken into three expanding focuses—*the Self, the Heart, and the Hands*—twenty-three perspectives in this book shed light on where classrooms and businesses meet. The wisdom is applicable to anyone in any role of either realm. Every chapter has a character code that the corporate world and education world value. What started out as a text for educators alone has now become a focal point for any employee at any company who wants to be the best he or she can be.

Ultimately, the more we can create students who are college-and career-ready, the more successful they (and the corporate world) will be. The only way we can ever possibly hope to narrow the divide is by building relationships with each other to foster a great truth, a higher purpose, and—eventually—happier and more successful people, relationships, and organizations.

What is the role of a teacher? It is no different from that of a CEO.

Acknowledgments

To everyone who escalated this book into an enlightening project that connects the perspectives and wisdom of inspirational people, to everyone who supported and encouraged the ideas and the writing, to friends and family who believed in its purpose, thank you!

—Joy

To my family and friends,

No day goes by where we are not thankful to those who motivated us to continue to move forward, despite any obstacle that stood in our way. Thank you for always believing that, by shooting for the stars, we'd at least reach the moon.

—Tony

Introduction

The text is sectioned into three broadening perspectives including twenty-one chapters of concise stories, poignant discussions, and practical advice. In addition, each chapter includes real-world assistance for teachers and business leaders and practical advice for both parties. Although each chapter can be explored separately, it would be helpful to review each section in order, as references are made to previous chapters and the overall development is sequential in nature.

Sharing Mindsets: Where Classrooms and Businesses Meet establishes a journey from the self, to the heart, to the hands, magnifying one's own potential and subsequently magnifying the potential in others. The premise resides in each of us, no matter the position; we have leadership qualities that, when discovered and applied, assist not only us, but the organization as a whole.

Part I, "An Inward Journey of the Self," encourages the examination of the self as a starting point of influence. Advice and wisdom from education and business leaders prompt a personal introspective probing that solidifies an attitude and mindset for successful interactions. In this fashion, once we establish a solid foundation for success, the road on which we will travel to assist others becomes more possible.

Part II, "An Outward Journey of the Heart," identifies the keys to building and sustaining relationships in classrooms, schools, and businesses. An emphasis on empowering, motivating, and appreciating others cultivates an environment worth working in every day. The key to any relationship is being able to relate to another; we do this by using all of our senses, particularly our hearts, to first establish the basis of a connected perspective.

Part III, "An Impactful Journey of the Hands," outlines the broadest influence of the self, the generous extension into the community—breaking through the walls of the workplace out to the local and greater communities with intention of service is a lifelong gift. Giving may be the single, greatest act of humanity so long as the act comes without the expectation of affirmation. Through this text, one can create a secure foundation upon which generosity becomes the sanctuary to a more purposeful, fulfilling life.

The text concludes with the notion that if one can set in motion the self, the heart, and the hands, then these prime ideals can guide a life of magnanimous prosperity and happiness. Being happy and accepting of one's self and others starts with understanding that happiness is not a place but an approach to all things good.

Part I
AN INWARD JOURNEY OF THE SELF

Before we can concentrate on extending our hearts, or extending our hands, we must first prioritize who we are with the understanding that the best way to bring out the best in others is to show up every day for life. Don't just get up and get there, but show up! By doing so, our ability to demonstrate positive influence will grant us the opportunity to develop both our hearts and our hands no matter what position we hold. We must own our self-pride to gain the momentum needed to be a positive force in our leadership and in life.

1

Just a Rough Launch, Not Going to Be a Bad Day!

Gain Momentum from Moments

> Knock (difficult tasks) out before 9:00 a.m. If you place the tough things toward the end of the day, your whole day is burdened by what is ahead.
>
> —Douglas C. Yearley Jr., *chairman and CEO, Toll Brothers*[1]

Teacher Ted Martin thought the sound of his 5:35 a.m. alarm on this fresh, September morning was simply divine. Summer had left him rejuvenated, and as usual, he was inspired on this first day of school to make a positive impact on his students. With this optimistic outlook, Ted literally jumped out of bed, ready to face the day with a confident spirit.

As usual, the morning routine was mentally layered with his daily intentions: the science lesson he would begin today, the union meeting he needed to schedule for later in the week, the copies of assessments he needed to run for Thursday, and the students he taught last year whom he promised to connect with at lunch. All of these objectives ran through his mind, while he simultaneously prepared for the morning jaunt.

As he bounced to the kitchen to seize his java, he was instantly aggravated to see that the coffee pot had overflowed, spilling grounds and coffee onto the counter. In fact, the dribbles of murky stains had already begun to make their way down the front of the cabinets.

Ted thought to himself, "Sure would be nice to ignore the mess and hit the local coffee shop, but I don't have time to take the longer route today with everything I want to accomplish." In the most efficient way, Ted dumped the coffee, started running water through the pot to clean out the grounds, and began the process of resetting the coffee pot, a déjà vu event from the previous evening.

The cleanup added several minutes to his morning, but Ted was confident that catastrophe had been avoided. Unfortunately, that feeling was short-lived. Turning to start breakfast, he realized he had completely neglected the needs of his dog, Lucky. In fact, not only did Lucky's whine convey his displeasure, but he also left a surprise puddle by the back door. The soggy cleanup continued.

Ted's vision of how smoothly the morning would go had vanished as his mind began to shift into a negative state. Unfortunately, here is where his customary voice began its all too familiar chant, "I wish I could just go in late today. If I could only win the lottery, I would not have to work at all. Maybe I'll just call in sick."

Later, but not late, he managed to go from his house to his car and eventually to school. However, even as he arrived and was greeted by students and staff, it was evident to everyone that Ted's morning did not go as planned. In fact, everyone received at least a snippet of the events that occurred within the morning's struggle. It was barely 7:35 a.m., and the day was already marked as a disaster.

Imagine your day unfolding in a similar manner as Ted's. Of course, we've all had mornings like this, where the choice of handling the day's events comes with either a positive or a negative stance. However, too often we choose the negative path and minor moments escalate us to our boiling point. But why?

Humans make emotional decisions; the key is to use moments that ignite us, as they are critical to our personal empowerment. We can and do possess the choice to gain momentum from our moments and allow them to propel us forward, or choose to allow them to cause a trailing attitude. Moments make up the story of our lives, and every moment matters. **We have the power to decide how much weight to assign to those moments.**

Doug Yearley, CEO of Toll Brothers, was the perfect choice to represent this chapter and the idea of "owning" our moments. While speaking with Doug, we were intrigued by his ability to focus on the self when it came to his demeanor. Doug stated, "But there are times that I come in here in a bad mood, and I have to be mindful of that. I have to be aware of my emotional state. In my position, I [have to be] mindful of how I act and how people will react to [my mood]." This type of self-awareness (the ability to realize the impact of your disposition on others) is the launch pad for owning moments and building a solid foundation for others.

Think back to our friend Ted. Ted chose to allow the coffee and pet disaster to define his morning and, more importantly, to taint all future interactions and events. As he chose to engage his colleagues in his misery, the spiral continued—bringing about more insurmountable challenges that could not readily be conquered. **Many times, we find ourselves in a "powerless" position.** However, when we really examine the situation, more times than not, we have placed ourselves in that position by choice.

Doug believes that this type of self-selection—"feeling miserable"—hurts not only ourselves but our colleagues as well. "I think you need to be very mindful of your own state and how to get through it so it doesn't impact others. I may be serious or concerned about something, but I don't want it to affect my demeanor. We must lead by example, and if we do that enough, we build a culture where we all have less gloomy days."

Rick Hanson, neurophysicist and co-author of *Buddha's Brain: The Practical Neuroscience of Happiness, Love, and Wisdom*, scientifically supports focusing on the positive and aligns with Doug's self-selection mindset. Hanson reminds us, "Each of us has two wolves in the heart, one of love and one of hate. Everything depends on which one we feed each day."[2]

Positive events, actions, and moments springboard and propel people and companies forward; these moments are critical to success on numerous levels.

If the negative moments of the day are indeed causing you to be negative, then maybe a change is necessary in order for you to help people in your life to another level. For example, did you know that Doug was a lawyer prior to becoming the CEO of Toll Brothers? Fact is, in Doug's words, he "hated it," as the fight in litigation was causing negativity. Doug took a chance and threw his hat in the ring for his current position. Lucky for Doug, his dad had always taught him to be handy, thus, hand skills paired with a legal background gave him the experience needed for a chance at his current job. Therefore, there are times when change is necessary.

Now, should someone like our friend Ted Martin quit teaching because of spilled coffee? Probably not. However, if the negativity one feels at the little things is masking a bigger issue, then perhaps a serious audit of one's life is necessary. In other words, do not spend your life wishing you were doing your first job while you are in your second one. That is a tough way to live and, ultimately, a recipe for negativity and regret.

To create a recipe for optimism, we must train our brains to establish a mindset that colors events more positively. In this fashion, we can recreate the rest of our moments as positive forces, which gain momentum *for good*, for ourselves and for others. Being positive does not have to be an event-to-event occurrence. It's a mindset.

Choose wisely.

THE FOCUSED SELF: OWN YOUR MOMENTS

Can you define yourself as having a *rough launch* versus a *bad day*? Discipline your heart to give positive weight to those events and actions that are going to move you in a direction that is best for yourself and for your colleagues. Imagine beginning the day with an optimistic outlook and a humorous perspective on your morning launch. Perhaps peers and students do not even recognize that you had a bad morning. More so, perhaps they feel confident and comfortable to ask you and tell whatever is on their heart because they see you as secure, unburdened, and willing to tackle the feats of the day.

Begin to see life as a series of moments that matter and tell your story, but also see yourself as the author of that story. Be selective about the moments you carry with you throughout the day and those that are left behind. Your daily stamina and momentum to get through a day are best propelled by an optimistic outlook and a positive pool of events.

Likewise, develop strategies that help you *gain* momentum during the day instead of losing it. For example, Doug's title quote, "Knock out [difficult tasks] before 9:00 a.m. If you place the tough things toward the end of the day, your whole day is burdened by what is ahead," provides one brilliant way to turn your focus toward owning the positive of the day instead of the negative. We all have parts of our jobs that are difficult, and sometimes, the natural reaction is to procrastinate on exactly these parts. But, as CEOs, or teachers, or shelf stockers, if we are able to prioritize our tasks and handle the not-so-pleasant items first, we may be able to ignite the positivity that comes with accomplishment.

NOTES

1. All Douglas C. Yearley Jr. quotes presented in this chapter are from an in-person interview with the authors that took place on April 27, 2018.

2. Rick Hanson, *Buddha's Brain: The Practical Neuroscience of Happiness, Love, and Wisdom* (Oakland, CA: New Harbinger Publications, 2009), 133.

2

What D'ya Mean I Can't Redo the Day?

Honor Life's Brevity

> It is very hard to get where you want to go if you do not know where that is!
>
> —H. Edward Hanway, *former CEO, Cigna Corporation*[1]

Have you noticed the increasing popularity of Word Art? Instead of finding paintings of floral arrangements and landscapes in home decor, we encounter words in a variety of fonts, sizes, and colors shouting out our messages on painted walls and in framed works. We think about who we are and the character traits that we prioritize, then we announce them in word art or even in an organized shape such as a *Wordle*. (For those of you who are unfamiliar, *Wordle* is one of many online tools used for generating "word clouds.") Words typically associated with each other are put into the program by the user; an informative image can be created to further emphasize the meaning of the words. In thinking about this visualization, have you ever created a word art image of yourself?

Melanie Foster is an insurance agent, and during a recent conversation with a few of her teacher clients, she was reminded why her work matters so much.

John Smythe, an earth science teacher, shared one of his favorite lessons with Melanie. John was teaching his students about Earth and explained to them, "Planet Earth is approximately 4.5 billion years old. The sun is midway through its lifespan at almost 5 billion years." Initially, the students seemed unimpressed by the numbers, but the reality started to sink in when the conversation turned to relativity. "When the sun's life is extinguished, Earth will follow shortly thereafter."

John subsequently asked the students what they believed was the average lifespan of a person; most students shouted out 100 years. (The luxury of technology enabled someone else to yell out a more realistic number.)

"Seventy-eight years," one boy bellowed.

John applauded the boy's efforts and then asked them to imagine a symbol of seventy-eight years on a scale of Earth's current age of 4.5 billion years. What would that look like in comparison? The most microscopic concept they could tangibly conjure up was a grain of sand or salt. To that, John intensified the conversation and asked them if they realized the miniscule amount of time a human life has compared to the time Earth offers. Ultimately, one or two students paused and then mustered a response such as, "Wow! We are grains of sand on Earth's huge desert."

"Yes," John stated, "and knowing the small time we have, we need to appreciate and value every moment."

As Melanie Foster sat through this short lesson, she could feel the goose bumps on her neck rise. She thought to herself, "We are all important and valued and each of us has an unidentified length of time on Earth to make life happen." Be it home or auto, her job was to ensure that her clients felt that, although we might scientifically be particles in this vast land, none of us need to feel so small. She valued her clients' feeling of security and trust. And this is why folks felt compelled to use her as an insurance agent and as a friend. Each client mattered to her much like each moment mattered to her, and, if she could convey this genuine spirit to her peers, the "selling" would take care of itself.

The phrase "life is short" is habitually tossed around in conversation as a justification for living life extravagantly or taking a risk. Yet, perhaps we should approach every day with the attitude that life is short and let it be a beacon for all our interactions and activities. There have been countless lives before us and there will be countless lives after; however, in our distracted hurriedness, we still seem to undervalue the moments and the rarity of each day.

But what causes this? Sometimes, we allow ourselves to be designed and distorted by the circumstances and people around us. Conversely, we need to own our values and take charge of the small grain of life that we have been afforded. We do not have infinite time; therefore, we cannot afford to live with values that are irrelevant and do not shape us to the positive. Values such as clear communication, effective collaboration, humor, respect, discipline, and diligence might be a list we live by.

Ed Hanway, former CEO of Cigna, has a clear code that works for him; he shared, "I have always adhered to the idea that leadership requires three basic principles: Vision/Values, Communication, and Motivation." In a sense, Ed has summarized the entire premise of this chapter in a focused mantra: **time and interactions with people are limited each day; every day we decide not to hold true to our values is a day missed—for ourselves and for colleagues.**

Ed believes that "a leader needs to have a clear sense of what their purpose is and what they want to accomplish. They also must be clear as to how they want to achieve their vision." Furthermore, his position on communication follows perfect suit in that "effective communication requires a compelling and consistent articulation of vision and purpose. A message that inspires others and hopefully motivates them to see value in their efforts beyond just the completion of a specific task."

Yet it is his understanding of what motivated each team member that made him and his colleagues so successful. In other words, Ed realized that "vision and communication without the right people, who were as motivated to succeed as he was, would not work." Therefore, he took it upon himself to own the value of motivating others, as a true mark of infectious leadership in any company or classroom. And this type of spirit was critical to have every day.

For example, think about today. In life, this day on the calendar comes along once. It will not circle back around. We get one shot at maximizing who we are and giving our very best; life does not allow for rewinds or do overs. **You do not get a refund on the day if you choose to live it beneath your values.** As educators, workers, CEOs, and other similar roles, what we elect to do is impactful. **Our students and staff benefit most when the persona that we offer is defined by what is best for them.** It is critical that your persona is not influenced by negative circumstances or threatening environments. Specifically, your values need to hold up and hold true regardless of the weather, regardless of the weekday, and regardless of the other places you think you would rather be. You owe it to yourself and to your students/customers to live up to a code that stands up to the circumstances of life.

Values, not personality, should drive our daily behaviors and principles. Sometimes we become so focused on how we present ourselves to others through our personality that we undermine the importance of leading with our values. Companies such as Saxbys, a Philadelphia-based coffee shop business, paint their values on the walls of their corporate headquarters: *We are a Community Serving Our Community; Embrace Being O.D.D. (Outgoing, Detail Oriented, and Disciplined); Loyalty + Profitability = Growth; Live with Pride, Passion, and Purpose; Serve Yourself by Serving Others; Care Personally and Communicate Openly.*

Nick Bayer, CEO of Saxbys questions, "Why would you have personal core values and then choose to work for a company that has different values than you do? Why would you do that?"[2] It's a very good question to ponder. If our values are who we are, then those values cross all boundaries and we should possess values that are effective at home, in the community, in the office, and in the classroom; they resonate with our friends and our families.

On a daily basis, the challenges of a career test the personalities of us all. We need to develop and sustain a code of character that defies these demands. **We must build a code of character that exemplifies our appreciation and honors life that is limited and cannot be replayed or redone.**

Our emotional shape is defined by our values and attitudes; focus on who we are and create a code that outlines our interactions, decisions, and relationships. Our ability to be our daily best comes from the persona we create and shape; it is self-defined, not circumstantially or environmentally defined.

THE FOCUSED SELF: OWN YOUR VALUES

Can you hold steadfast to the person that you are, not allowing your persona to be negatively molded by people around you and circumstances you encounter? What is your identity code or word cloud of your key values? Do you revisit it numerous times throughout the day, and are you honest with yourself when you veer off track from who you are? It is okay. We are all human beings, and, sometimes, we all need a reset.

In our professions, we must discipline ourselves to maintain a value focus, being in charge of our own attitudes and outlooks through each interaction. Be aware, *now*-that time and interactions with people are limited, and responses from all folks are not in our control.

If we maintain a value list that is concise, yet comprehensive, it will be manageable to sustain. Think about values toward others such as acceptance, compassion, encouragement, honor, and passion. Make them visible to yourself as a reminder that your personal code will not be altered or rocked—hold solid to your code. Time is not on our side. Each day we decide not to hold true to our values is a day missed.

Remember Horace—*Carpe Diem*.

NOTES

1. All H. Edward Hanway quotes presented in this chapter are from a phone interview with the authors that took place on March 22, 2018.

2. This Nick Bayer quote, as well as those presented in chapter 18, are from an in-person interview with the authors that took place on June 14, 2018.

3

Become the Family Dog!

Personalize Your Behaviors

> When you try to be your best, it makes me want to be my best; it makes others want to be their best. In our culture, if we want to have a family business, and we want to have an impact on behaviors, we have to give to the best of our ability.
>
> —Ed Herr, *president and CEO, Herr Foods, Inc.*[1]

Ms. Hope Brightens was anything but her name. A self-proclaimed "realist," Hope brought neither the happiness of her name nor the hope of a brighter tomorrow to anything she did. Now, far be it from anyone to judge another person's disposition; folks do have the right to be miserable just as they have the choice to be exuberant. However, the problem that Ron Mercer had was that Hope was one of his customer service representatives, and the complaints from the customers were as endless as the horizon.

Ron knew that Hope did have several saving qualities; she was an efficient bookkeeper. She was able to multitask with the best of them and was a complete whiz when it came to technology.

Deep down, Ron knew he was sacrificing some of the consumer's "happiness" to attain such high performance. Once more, he knew Hope's colleagues avoided her like the flu. In fact, on many occasions, folks would turn the other way just to avoid making contact with her. Reliable employee. Tough personality.

Do you know anyone like Hope Brightens?

In today's world, this short vignette is not that far-fetched. (Heck, in life, folks come across these types of people daily.) The problem presents itself in the fact that the climate of the workplace is dictated by the attitude of the employee. In other words, how we act impacts others!

Ed Herr, of Herr Foods, Inc., is a man who truly knows how to treat others. If you spend a few moments with him, you can sense his genuine concern for others and his true spirit for making each experience with a person a positive encounter. Ed's words resounded with us when we thought about personalizing the behaviors, especially when we think about Hope's tale. What does it take to be nice to someone? We have all heard the phrase "it takes more muscles in our face to frown than to smile," but too often, we choose the scowl over the smile. But why?

Perhaps in our society, we have placed more emphasis on tasks instead of people. In Ed's words, "Probably the most commonly held thing about leadership or living life is loving people, whether loving your neighbor or whoever it is in your life. And I guess one of the best ways of loving people is when you see the good in them (tell them). So many times people look for faults today because we feel like it's the best way to turn things around."

In Ed's philosophy, a solid principle to learn and live by in life is to feed what is working. He suggests, "If you see people as potential, you say I'm going to look for the good in that person and water that, that's faster growth than any other kind of growth. If you find the faults in people and feed that, it's not going to give you the results that you want."

Ed does admit that "it takes more energy looking for the positives." In this statement, we find that getting to know someone on a personal level is not easy. In fact, it is not supposed to be, but the secret is when we place our behaviors second, and concentrate on the person in front of us, we establish and build trust. This trust leads to openness and a great starting point for a relationship.

It's easy to say to someone, especially our Ms. Hope Brightens, "Just be happy." But sometimes the act of this reality becomes clouded in the simplicity of the command. Perhaps a thought process is needed prior to adopting this mantra. For example, we once saw a quote that said, "Happiness is not a destination but a mindset." And for our money, no one bears more fruit for this ideal than our four-legged friend.

Consider this question: **After an absence of five minutes, five hours, or five days, how does your dog treat you?** Be it Fido, Betsy, or Rudy, your dog exhibits unconditional, genuine, boundless love for you each and every time you encounter. In fact, upon your return home from a stressful day, the *canine climate* seemingly erases all negatives and illuminates your attitude. Yes, just the simple run to your legs confirms your greatness as a human. Now, if you own a dog or not, the point still serves: The *canine climate* exemplifies the inclusive, appreciated feeling that you desire in yourself and in others.

Ed suggests that the secret to helping folks become better people is encouragement. "Everybody needs encouragement; there's a proverb that says, 'Anxious hearts are very heavy,' (we live in a world of anxiousness), but a word of encouragement works like magic. I think encouragement is what dogs do. They encourage us, they are happy to see us, and they only see the good."

As an educator or employee, your role would be effortless if everyone responded to your entrance the way a dog greets you in your home; a room full of wagging attitudes and eager, cheerful ears who welcome your words and actions. Our dogs believe we are people of purpose, love, generosity, zest, and enthusiasm. But are we?

This can be a very difficult question to answer for us all. Maybe you are that person only on Fridays or when the store is empty on a holiday? But if you climb inside the mind and heart of a dog, you come to understand that the dog does not evaluate or judge you based on any of those factors. Dogs love you regardless of circumstances and regardless of factors which are beyond their, and your, control. This is a critical point worth mentioning again: **The canine climate exists regardless of the other factors that lie outside human connections.**

For example, in the popular novel Marley and Me, John Grogan depicts a dog in this way:

> A dog has no use for fancy cars or big homes or designer clothes. Status symbols mean nothing to him. A water-logged stick will do just fine. A dog judges others not by their color or creed or class but by who they are inside. A dog doesn't care if you are rich or poor, educated or illiterate, clever or dull. Give him your heart and he will give you his.[2]

How many people can you say that about?

Are we the person our dog thinks we are? This honest question is a driving force behind personalizing our behaviors. Since we have little control over the behaviors and responses of those around us, we cannot expect people to respond to us the way we would. No matter your personal circumstances (and we all deal with tragedies in life) when we enter the arena, we must be willing and able to display a genuine passion for our craft and, most importantly, our students, and customers.

THE FOCUSED SELF: OWN YOUR BEHAVIORS

Ed Herr is a man of influence, much like each CEO we encountered. His thoughtful perspective on his position in our society was a real gem for the practical advice for leaders when it comes to owning our behaviors in our community.

In speaking of staying grounded, Ed stated that,

> What happens is people in my world, as an executive, whether its employees or people that come to visit me, they're really quick to tell you how great you are, for various reasons. They could be selling something, asking for money, asking for your time, so what happens automatically is that you think more highly of yourself than you really should. It's not healthy to always be around that sort of environment. So when you go out on the street, and you just experience real life, it just gives you a different perspective; it gives you a perspective on how your employees are feeling, how other people view life, or view you. And so by watering others, you water yourself . . . start pouring your life into people.

As Ed mentioned, if we own a business in the community or work in the school system, we are serving the very families that sustain our positions. As Ed stated, "Like at home, you want to take care of your family. (I want to) have a relationship with

1,300 people. 1,300 families. Our job is to nurture and care for them and build transparency which builds trust." In that regard, the trust we build extends from our values (intrinsic) to our behaviors (extrinsic). Here is where the *self* serves as a ladder to attain greater heights as leaders and as people.

There is no doubt it takes daily discipline, but when you enjoy it, you practice it and Ed honestly states, "You don't always feel like it, right? Sometimes you feel like eating another bag of chips or something!"

NOTES

1. All Ed Herr quotes presented in this chapter are from an in-person interview with the authors that took place on March 27, 2018.

2. John Grogan, *Marly & Me: Life and Love with the World's Worst Dog* (New York: William Morrow, 2005), 280.

4

At What Cost? And We Don't Mean Money!

Embrace Your Boundaries

> It takes a little bit of self-awareness and self-evaluation to really understand what your prescription can be. It's sort of like you go to the doctor, and she says what's wrong, and how she can help you. (Then she) writes a prescription. So you look at yourself, and say, 'What makes me happy? What gets me excited? What gives me a breath of fresh air?' Then you write that prescription (for yourself).
>
> —Rakia Reynolds, *founder and CEO, Skai Blue Media*[1]

Maggie Donahue prides herself in instructing 150 sixth-grade middle school math students in a day. If you ask any student, present or past, they would quickly associate Maggie with traits like dedicated, hardworking, caring, intelligent, organized, compassionate, and the list goes on. Outside of the classroom, Maggie chairs numerous school committees and makes great progress in school improvement. Be it a sport, an activity, or an event, Maggie's presence is as predictable as a one-sided coin flip. As one can tell, Maggie is very loyal; in return, she is cherished by students, staff, and families alike.

At home, Maggie has a young family—two elementary-aged children, a husband, and a huge Golden Shepard named Rudy. She has a beautiful house, one which exudes pride with its organization and cleanliness. The neighbors appreciate her on the homeowners' association, and she is always volunteering to bake brownies or cookies to meet the needs of social events. Beyond herself, she gives countless hours to her family members by making meals, being their personal Uber to their activities, and passionately attending their games and concerts. Some might say that Maggie does it all. Interestingly, we wonder what Maggie would say. Funny how no one has asked her!

One of the greatest assets in being a qualitative researcher is asking questions of folks to assist us in learning together. When we had a chance to sit and talk with Maggie (name changed), she stated that initially "she loved her job and family" as evidenced in the infinite hours she devoted to both. However, as we continued, Maggie hinted that she was not "as happy as folks thought." In the deeper dive, Maggie had mentioned that one of the stressors in her life was her belief that she "did not love herself." Unfortunately, Maggie expressed that she was "caught in the trap" that so many find themselves in. **Maggie had neglected boundaries in an effort to please everyone around her.**

In fact, as the conversation concluded, she was very quick to point out that she could not remember the last time she "went to the gym" or even just "visited friends." When asked, "When was the last time you got a break?" her response was simply a head shake, "Never."

Our ability to define ourselves and who we are is as important as defining how we spend our time—both are key to sustaining energy. Setting realistic personal limits, boundaries, and expectations is necessary to maximizing our potential. The boundaries must be flexible, and nothing (aside from emergencies) should be expended at the expense of our personal stamina. Think about it. **If *we* cannot get through a day, how are *we* going to be beneficial and valuable for anyone around us?**

Rakia Reynolds is the creative CEO and founder of multimedia public relations agency Skai Blue Media. Obviously, the undertakings of organizing this entire celebrated company can be exhausting. Like most CEOs (heck, like most of us that work), the job can seem like a 25/8 work week. (Yes, we realize the cliché is 24/7, but when we become really engaged, those extra hours turn into extra days.) While speaking with Rakia, we quickly learned that she is not only an amazing business woman but also an amazing person.

Aside from her vast inspirational, professional knowledge, one of her personal goals is self-preservation. In our discussion, Rakia stated, "If you are constantly torn down because you have over-extended yourself, and you over-serviced people, and you over-delivered, then you can't be your best self to anyone." Now, although some might believe that taking care of one's self limits our ability to help others, it actually helps to sustain our passion and purpose.

Unfortunately, over-achievers fall victim to a pattern of accomplishments for others; educators and others in service occupations are the frontrunners in this generosity race. After all, we give of ourselves, our intelligence, our emotions, and our time every day without built-in time for reflection or recuperation.

Hours run into family and personal time, and the day all too often feels like an exhausting race and not an inspiring journey. Rakia describes, "We have over 60,000 thoughts per day and my job is to really help myself to have at least 50,000 positive ones because you can easily have negative thoughts that enter your mind and that takes a lot of training and a lot of mental toughness. One of my clients, you know I have worked with Serena Williams for about 4 1/2 years, and she said to me once, 'mental toughness is not found in an aisle at CVS, it is something you have to build over time.' And that is something that always stuck with me. So it's having that frame of mind from the time that I get up in the morning until I go to sleep but my brain is going to have 60,000 thoughts today and it's my job to make sure that at least 50,000 of them are positive thoughts or thoughts of affirmation or thoughts of productivity. That type of mental toughness takes daily discipline and daily mindfulness!"

As human beings, we become physically and emotionally eroded prioritizing the expectations of others and neglecting our own boundaries. Research professor and author Brene Brown conceptually identifies, "Daring to set boundaries is about having the courage to love ourselves even when we risk disappointing others."[2]

Key words in her statement are critical to its adoption. *Daring* to set boundaries implies that it is not an easy feat; it is not something that everyone is comfortable doing. Think about activities in life that are categorized as daring; they often precede with "I dare you to . . . go on that treacherous roller coaster, try that pizza with snails and sausage, ask that beautiful person to dance, go into that dark bat-laden cave alone." All of those potential events come with a smidgen of trepidation and great contemplation.

When you *dare* to set boundaries, know that it is a decision that will not come easy, but the reward on the other side is potentially amazing; one might love the intimidating roller coaster, the pizza might become your new favorite flavor, one dance might become a lifelong relationship, and maybe you love bats after all.

How do you know if you don't try?

Rakia's comments also echo Brown's research. When chatting about our personal selves, Rakia confirmed, "And I would say I have probably had more of a reactive way of dealing with it for the mental health and the physical health because I wanted to preserve everything that I had, not only because you love yourself, because typically as a parent, you love yourself last. You love your family first, you love your kids first. If your kids have to go to the doctor you make sure those things are done whether it's telling your husband or calling and setting those things up and then you put yourself last."

How true! When we discussed this quote among ourselves, we have to admit it really hit home. We are both so family oriented that sometimes we "lose our own identity" within the framework of our tasks. In other words, it is too easy for Tony to become dad to Brett, Braden, and Brad; husband to Denise; son of Skip and Rose; and so on instead of being Tony. Same is true for Joy (obviously with different children, parents, and so on).

In life, it becomes so critical for us to have folks that can and do help us to help ourselves. As Rakia articulated, "We are as good as the company we keep." In this fashion, when we revisit our beginning story, we wished Maggie had someone to assist her in loving herself. It is critical to have support systems in place that allow us the time and energy to set our boundaries for our clients, students, and families, as well as for ourselves.

Brown also identifies that we must embrace the "courage to love ourselves." This is not to be confused with selfishness. It is not selfish to have the courage to draw lines in the sands of life when the payoff is our personal stamina. We can go farther and do more by setting boundaries and having the courage to say I love who I am and who I need to be for others. And sometimes, all we need is a break in the action of the moment.

As Rakia explains, "Sometimes I need to get up to take a fifteen minute walk around the block, or sometimes it's five minutes or sometimes it's a quick three minute walk, but I have been able to expose myself to some sort of air or sunshine, and those are things that make me happy." Again, Maggie's generosity is admirable as long as it is not at the expense of her love for herself. At some point, she will question the giving and begin to wonder where her own identity has gone. This focus is the "prescription" that Rakia mentioned in our opening quote.

Like a physician, we have to be willing and able to recommend the right amount of "self-love" for our own existence to remain positive and productive.

Has Maggie sacrificed who she is to be boundless for others? Do you?

THE FOCUSED SELF: OWN YOUR BOUNDARIES

Ask yourself this question, "At what expense am I accomplishing everything I do?" "Suffering" is a strong word, but it seems to be fitting to question what is suffering in your life while everyone else is reaping the rewards of *you*. Take time and answer that question and adopt an approach that is inclusive yet protective. When asked to participate or give time to an activity or event, have the *courage* to say I can give fifteen minutes but not thirty, I can help out on Saturday, but not on Sunday, I can't do . . . but I can do . . . Rakia extends this one step further, "I am training myself to say *no* without explanations now because I know myself. I am just not going to give an explanation at all, but it will just be shorter. So now if I say, Rakia, say no without an explanation, the explanation will just be shorter, it's just having that frame of mind of like giving yourself parameters with the no's."

Using powerful statements that identify what you are willing to do, but courageously stating what you cannot do will enable you to honor yourself and love who you are. At the end of the day, others will see that illumination that exudes from within you; despite all the demands and all the giving, you still embrace yourself and love the person you are.

Speaking of powerful statements, one of the last pieces of advice we garnered from our visit with Rakia was this modest, yet powerful, message:

> I don't think there is a black and white answer; we live in the gray, all of us live in the gray, and it's finding out what are our points of happiness. What are the things that make us happy? Some people might say it's not spending a whole bunch of time with family; it might be taking a walk every day. I think we have to look at what are the ten things that make us happy. What are the ten things that get us excited; what are the ten things that help you feel like you have a breath of fresh air. Then, just make sure we are incorporating them more frequently in our lives.

Well said, Rakia. Well said.

NOTES

1. All Rakia Reynolds quotes presented in this chapter are from a phone interview with the authors that took place on June 15, 2018.

2. Brené Brown's "3 Ways to Set Boundaries," *O, The Oprah Magazine,* September 2013 issue; also available on Oprah.com: http://www.oprah.com/spirit/how-to-set-boundaries-brene-browns-advice.

5

Call Your Own Timeout in Your Life Game!

Assess and Recalibrate

> There is only so much you can control in a situation; to get ourselves all out of sorts because an interaction didn't go our way does not make a ton of sense.
>
> —Gary Jonas Jr., *president, The HOW Group*[1]

What do you see in the following picture?

If you answered an "X," you are not alone. In fact, majority of folks answered in the same fashion. In knowing that with art, there truly are no wrong answers, the conversation could stop there. However, did you know that artists sometimes creatively use spaces in their artwork that are not taken up by the main subject of their renderings? In effect, they utilize negative space as a valuable contribution to the overall artwork. As crowded or empty as the piece may seem, there is space for more meaningful contour with or without actual artistry.

Now, please go back and take another look. Do you see the gray? The three boxes? The unused space? Get the picture? (Pun intended.)

Similarly, **we all have negative spaces in our daily that offer pockets of time that we can utilize as valuable contributions to our day.** Yet, in wanting to be "productive members of society," we are conditioned to keep going. For example, how often do you find yourself answering the question "How are you?" with a response such as, "Good, but busy" or just "Busy!" or just "Good" (followed by a list of the things keeping you busy). **Regrettably, most of us are validated by the lists that define the minutes of our day.**

Do the following adages hold true for you? *Productivity equivocates success; busy people are meaningful people; a "To Do" list indicates purpose.* Simultaneously, in wanting to be productive, we keep our minds moving, blinding us to any negative space that could recalibrate our energy and emotions. Downtime seems to diminish once the day begins and the bell rings, and rings, and rings.

Gary Jonas of The HOW Group, a property development group based in Philadelphia, knows the value of hard work. In his organization, one of his stated maxims is that of securing that the work gets accomplished. "If you're going to work here, here's a couple of things that you need to know. Number one is, if it's your job, it's your job to get it done. And if it's not your job, it's your job to get it done. Whatever it takes for you to get from here to here, you have to get it done." As one can tell, the value of determined work is one that HOW prides itself upon.

In today's society, we talk a ton about grit factor. Hard work possesses much power in accomplishing our goals. In simple terms, those who are persistent tend to attain success when it comes to their endeavors. However, having grit to accomplish one's goal doesn't mean that there won't be times when we need to take a break from the challenge. Although we believe in the power of sustaining the passion and purpose for one's performance, we also believe in the value that comes with reassessing our situation when necessary.

In education, this concept is utilized in every classroom across the world. Students consistently hit the reset button when performance tends to wane. This notion makes perfect sense, as this is what we teach them to do. Yet, do we, as adults, follow the same thinking for ourselves?

As leaders, when we find ourselves in difficult, emotional moments, we must find a way to refocus our efforts, for *productivity is nothing without focus*. In his interview, we simply loved Gary's advice in this section: "If something went wrong for us, it's all about five minutes. We say, 'you have five minutes.' Go outside and, yell, scream, do whatever you have to do and then come back refocused and prepared for whatever it is that you have to do. Everybody deserves to get the best version of YOU they can get."

The tactic of refocusing is seen time and again in our culture. For example, one of our favorite, timeless movies is *The Hustler* starring Paul Newman and Jackie

Gleason.[2] In this classic 1961 film, both men portray pool sharks trying to outduel each other in a furious match. At one point in the movie, the action is fierce. Paul, playing the part of Fast Eddie Felson, tries to compensate for his frail emotional state by playing faster; however, Jackie's character, Minnesota Fats, takes a calculated break. He goes to the washroom to gain his composure. Upon returning, Minnesota calmly shuts the door on Fast Eddie's run. Rack 'em. Game over for Eddie.

If pool is not your game, perhaps another sport or activity serves point. In most, there are strategic actions one can take to regain the upper hand in a match or competition. One such strategy involves the antithesis of action; it is called the timeout.

Does the term "Ice the Kicker" mean anything to you? For a football fan, this term is slang for the use of a timeout by an opposing coach to cause a disruption to the kicker's rhythm by calling a timeout. By calling a calculated timeout, the hope of the opposing coach is to cause the kicker to "overthink" the kick, and, therefore, ultimately miss it because he or she put too much thought into a mostly muscle memory action. Does it work? Sometimes, but the fact remains that taking a timeout in sports or in life is a valuable way to give yourself time in tense situations.

Be it as an educator or property developer, we need to assess and recalibrate throughout the work day, as keeping our momentum high places us at our best for clients. It is too easy in a day to get caught in the spiral of bad moments only to realize the many victims of our negative attitude who had nothing to do with the original problem or conflict. For instance, think back to chapter 1, differentiating between a rough launch and a bad day. There is personal power in our ability to cap moments that mentally and emotionally erode us so we can be open to rebuilding ourselves.

In a day, the more often we can look at a moment as just that, a moment, and not escalate it and allow it to animate itself, the better we will be for ourselves and for others. Challenges are not going to stay away in a day, but we can choose to be disciplined and reset ourselves to avoid the pile up.

In speaking with Gary, we learned much about his values and how they fit into the self. In being educators, we chatted about education, and the impact teachers have on student lives. One of our favorite moments from our conversation rose when Gary stated that "we have to do our job as if the person we respect the most in the world is sitting on our shoulders and watching us work every day saying, 'I am proud of the way you performed today.'"

We were so inspired by this statement, not just as educators, but as human beings with a belief that work should be accomplished without the plaudits. No matter what position we hold, if we believe that our work is making someone else proud, we then have the ability to pass that pride onto the next person. In other words, we "do" the job the right way even when no one is watching because someone (ourselves) is always witnessing our efforts. In schools, we call this doing it for the mirror.

We all have the ability to enlighten someone else's mind, to lift someone else's heart. But to be at our best, we have to be in the right mental framework to make that difference. In other words, when we concentrate on the self, we must realize that our ability to maintain the opportunity resides in our ability to secure the moment- without the recognition.

One successful strategy in this game of calming is self-talk. In education and business, we may have limited time to converse with our colleagues, but we do have time with ourselves, and we need to take advantage of that. Walking through the front door in the morning can either be a motivating conversation in our head or it can be a devastating discussion, whereby we focus on the tasks of the day, dreading the many factors that are out of our control (it's only Tuesday; I have a late meeting; it's cold and rainy; I wish I had a better lunch than a peanut butter sandwich . . . and more time to eat it).

The conversations upstairs that occur throughout the course of the day should take a positive pathway. These honest conversations we have with ourselves are critical to our ability to manage our social, physical, and emotional well-being. We do not necessarily have to recite daily affirmations in our brain with positive talk.

By constantly assessing and reassessing, we hold the power in identifying when to say when. In Gary's words, "I look at reframing situations into opportunities. If you are a "do whatever it takes" person with the right mindset, and you are positive, people are going to want to come to us and work with us, and we're going to grow." *Reframing situations* is a core strategy to bringing your best for others throughout the day.

THE FOCUSED SELF: OWN YOUR ASSESSMENT

As a start, try to locate the *negative spaces* within the rendering of your day where you can have conversations in your mind that are uplifting and are not detrimental to your productivity. It is surprising to discover the number of times in a day that are solely for you and are not shared with anyone else. Focus on utilizing those times to assess where you are emotionally and physically, and recalibrate yourself to be your best for you and your team.

In a day, there are pockets in your morning routine: driving to work, preparing for the day, in between meetings, lunch, walking the halls and stairwells, and so on that are conducive for this strategy. If you seek out extensive lengths of time, you will find yourself disappointed, as there are few of those in a busy person's schedule. Instead, seek out pockets of a minute or two minutes and seize those as maximizing moments to clear your thinking and recalibrate yourself. You will discover that you don't need long breaks in a day to refuel if you take advantage of the smaller windows of time.

In closing, we must remember Gary's point about being the best we can be. "Every person deserves our best!" In fact, we believe that every single person deserves everybody's best. If we all operated that way, the world would be different. So, if you are not feeling your best, take a break and prepare yourself for the next great moments of life.

NOTES

1. All Gary Jones quotes presented in this chapter are from an in-person interview with the authors that took place on September 7, 2018.
2. *The Hussler* (film, 1961, dir. Robert Rossen).

6

Be the Giving Tree, but First Water Your Roots!

Be Selfish to Be Generous

> We are only going to be able to take care of our patients when we have the state of mind to be there for them.
>
> —Andrea Gilbert, *president, Bryn Mawr Hospital*[1]

All employees of any company should be in the "giving" business. In other words, at the center of what we do should be a service-minded approach. Obviously, educators and caretakers should radiate this approach to our day! It is what we do. Be it for a child or a patient, helping others is at the heart of our central mission. And although the generosity we demonstrate on a daily basis is laudable, it can sometimes sap the energy that we possess to sustain our own happiness.

Have you ever found yourself saying, "Am I really going to make it through the day?" or "I simply cannot give anymore?" Likewise, are there times when Eeyore's "Oh, brother" mentality takes control of your thought patterns? We know there are days where only by cloning ourselves might we have the chance to please everyone's wishes (and that may not get it done either). It's true—the pail of generosity seems to empty quickly, leaving little left for ourselves or our personal lives.

To that end, the concept of "sympathetic selfishness" becomes a critical component for the sole purpose of fueling greater generosity. In other words, if we can prioritize to meet our own personal needs, then we will have the spirit and energy to give endlessly to others. Andrea Gilbert, president of Bryn Mawr Hospital, is the type of person that understands the benefit of being present in one's position. "Having staff who are focused, being nonjudgmental, and empathetic is part of being a good clinician." And Andrea sees her role as important in creating the type of climate that supports this environment: "At Bryn Mawr Hospital, we realize that caregivers give their best when they are in a supportive and safe environment." This reality has led to staff-centered initiatives including quiet respite rooms for staff, healthy food options, and facilitated conversations, where staff members can share their experiences for support. These initiatives contribute to providing a more desirable, balanced work environment. In jobs today, folks are asked to be flexible, as the market and tasks are ever-changing. However, this type of flexibility can take its toll on the mind, body, and spirit.

In the early 1950s, Art Clokey created a clay animated character named Gumby. Gumby's malleability enabled him to be pulled and twisted, shaped, and molded. The bendable figure was commercially available decades after its origination. In looking back at this childhood toy, it is now easy to relate to it metaphorically. Whereas the pulling and twisting in childhood was purely for entertainment and enjoyment, the pulling and twisting in adulthood is burdensome, stressful, and downright exhausting for staff that is in constant demand.

Think of how often in a day you feel like Gumby.

Most times, we cannot possibly imagine being stretched and pulled any farther for the benefit of our students, our patients, our peers, or for our own families. Secretly (and sometimes not so secretly), there are times that we crave a break or reprieve to recoil back into shape. Unfortunately, for those who never get the chance to recoil, the hopelessness starts to distort the very effort of being generous.

Shel Silverstein, in his children's book *The Giving Tree* has also mastered the concept of expensive generosity.[2] In this masterwork, the tree supplies so much to its owner that it becomes a shell of itself. If you know this story, you realize that giving is fantastic, but giving over what you can afford can sometimes blank our own ability to sustain.

Stretching—like *The Giving Tree* or Gumby—is virtually unavoidable as a caregiver (or any employee who takes on this mindset). For example, research has shown that teachers have 10,000 to 15,000 social interactions each week! We would venture that caregivers and public-facing employees have similar numbers. Let's face it, we are never going to be able to alleviate the daily demands placed upon us, but what we *can* change is our ability to handle those demands with energy and poise.

As Andrea noted, "patients respond to their caregivers when they can relate to them and when they feel like they're human." And one of the ways in which we can ensure that relatability is by maintaining a positive frame of mind.

Being selfish definitively connotes negativity coupled with a lack of concern for others; "sympathetic selfishness", however, can ignite personal generosity when the sculpting of who we are can serve a greater intention. **Giving to others is easy to do when you have first given to yourself.** Consider the following anecdote:

Mrs. Jody McClure was a tremendous nurse and person. In fact, she was everyone's "go to" person. Need a shoulder to cry on, see Jody. Need a hand with the rounds, Jody can help. Need a person to sponsor a health fair, Mrs. McClure would be there. In fact, at one point early in her career, Jody was on seven different hospital committees. Yes, seven! However, as time progressed, so did Jody's life outside of work. She eventually got married and started a family. She still was that same giving human being, but the demands on the outside had changed, and therefore, decisions had to be made.

One by one, Jody started to give up her committee leads. Although she was not happy about those decisions, she knew that her family was growing and needed their mom. Interestingly, the community did not witness such empathy. Quietly, folks started to question her commitment to the cause. Sure, her close friends realized the progression that life takes for colleagues, but not everyone did, especially the administration. Instead of the compassion that one would expect, some held it against her that the hospital was not number one in her life anymore.

Obviously, we know this would never be the case at Bryn Mawr Hospital, but there are places where this type of situation can occur. We share this short anecdote not to highlight the negative behavior of some but to be able to demonstrate that life changes, and, if we do not take time to focus on what is most important to us, we will not be the same person to those who depend on us the most.

Jody needed some time for herself. In having a family and a demanding career, those forty-five minutes of fitness were critical to her mental well-being. And although she could have stayed for senior club or mentorship meetings, she understood that without being a little selfish, she would not be the mother or nurse she wanted to be.

Andrea, too, realizes this type of thinking takes courage and discipline. "You have to put some important structure and boundaries around your commitments and your life so that you are available." Jody's discipline allowed her to carve out the necessary time to be a great mom, wife, nurse, peer, and friend.

Can we selfishly sculpt our lives to have greater intention and zest for others? Imagine the energy and heartfelt actions we can cast from a personality that is unpressured, uncomplicated, and secure. **The power to ignite others easily illuminates when we first ignite ourselves.** Being sympathetically selfish yields to a perfectly healthy *To Do* list: exercise, read a book, volunteer, call a friend, read an article, meditate, take a walk.

If we are going to empty our pail for others, we need to first fill it for ourselves.

THE FOCUSED SELF: OWN YOUR TIME

Prioritize yourself and the activities that fuel your day. When you create a mental or physical *To Do* list, include at least one charge for yourself that is energizing for your stamina and your zeal. Dropping off dry cleaning that is yours is certainly for you, but ask yourself how that is really igniting your value and your worth.

Likewise, be accepting of activities that vary on the days that seem saturated. You might be able to fit ten minutes of jumping jacks in as a workout in between your work and home schedule. *Something is better than nothing* is an acceptable approach. Consider filling your personal fuel tank in before the work day; you might be surprised to see how much your stamina improves if you start your day off with something you wanted—that will give you the ability to give to others the rest of the day. Begin to steer clear of statements such as *I don't have time* and take control of who you are; make the time!

Likewise, remember Andrea's advice in that we must be able to "unburden" ourselves of distractors that can hinder our ability to locate the balance necessary for success. We can't be unburdened because we can't always *eliminate* our burdens, but we can have an *outlook that's unburdened*, and that's a big difference.

In other words, both a work balance and a work-life balance are critical to creating an attitude of generosity, whereby we look to adjust our attitude to focus on what is within our control while we allow others to do their jobs as well. Be it the caregiver business or any work, our job as leaders is to equip our people with as many tools to refine their attitude as possible so that they can focus on their primary function with a positive spirit and energy worth catching.

NOTES

1. All Andrea Gilbert quotes presented in this chapter are from a phone interview with the authors that took place on April 23, 2018.
2. Shel Silverstein, *The Giving Tree* (New York: Harper & Row, 1964).

7

Life's Not Meeting You Halfway, Go Out and Get It!

Let Your Attitude Be the Catalyst

> You have to reinvent the way you do things or the way (they were) done. Create new ways to do the same thing. So I created a new way to sell French fries.
>
> —Pete Ciarrocchi, *chairman and CEO, Chickie's & Pete's Crab House and Sports Bar*[1]

Attitude is not just an outward appearance or a series of phrases—it's a mindset; it's a belief that you are a moving, positive force that will not be hindered by obstacles and challenges. Ignition does not stop at *I think I can* but drives for *I know I will* and moves directionally and confidently toward greatness. By possessing an igniting attitude, an educator holds the power to be a positive catalyst for students and peers alike.

In residing in Philadelphia, we have both been immersed in *Underdog* culture. From the images of Rocky Balboa ascending the Art Museum's steps to our modern underdog Nick Foles hoisting the Lombardi trophy for the World Champion Philadelphia Eagles, believing in one's self, even when everyone else does not, has been a battle cry for the ages.

We know there are those right now saying that this is nonsense. But the truth is, you can cultivate an attitude to be honorable and glorified, living each day with a winning mindset that breeds success. For example, let's examine the story of Sylvester Stallone and the Rocky Balboa character.[2]

As stated, Rocky is a cultural icon, symbolizing the grit that resides in us all; however, the Stallone story in itself did not start out so magnanimous. Early in life, Stallone contended with bullying, divorce, his own rebellious nature, poverty, and homelessness. Legend has it that, in desperation, Stallone sold his loyal canine companion for a measly amount of money, driving a stake of sadness and loss right through his own heart.

But thankfully for us, quitting was not an option. Like a perfectly written script of victory, he rose up against the obstacles, finally obtaining a contract and lead role for the Rocky film that he personally wrote. The most heartwarming turn of events occurred when he found and bought back the dog he had sold; the reunion of Stallone and his much loved companion solidified a sense of accomplishment.

The Rocky series of films went on to mimic a similar journey, attracting crowds and audiences who became inspired, leaving theaters with a hopeful, optimistic outlook for all facets of life. As the actor behind the lead character (and later in the series, a director as well, Sylvester Stallone has said, "That's what Rocky is all about: pride, reputation, and not being another bum in the neighborhood."[3] It's the true heroic tale of how you can go from *no one* to someone with gusto, intention, perseverance, and diligence.

Stallone further encourages us to wage the wars of daily life: "I believe there is an inner power that makes winners or losers. And the winners are the ones who really listen to the truth of their hearts."[4] An ignited heart with a passion and a drive for more, for greater, for better, for things to be above and beyond where they were yesterday makes a powerful tool in life and in the classroom. Stallone fought through obstacles his entire life and those obstacles paved his journey with a courageous, passionate, driven heart. **Imagine acquiring those traits and passionately approaching students every day with a *Rocky* attitude.**

If we look close enough, there are modern-day Rockys all around us who embody the "never say die" attitude. One such person is Pete Ciarrocchi, the CEO of Chickie's & Pete's. When speaking with Pete, we learned that his story holds similar parallels to Stallone. From humble beginnings, Pete was able to fight through his challenges and all of the naysayers who believed he was crazy for trying to change the establishment. One such person was his father:

> My father said to me, "What are you doing with these French fries? You're calling them crab fries?"
>
> I said, "Yea. I put seasoning on them; I made this seasoning [myself]."
>
> My dad said, "You made seasoning?"
>
> I said again, "Yea. You know the seasoning we put the crabs in, well I adjusted that and I did some other things to it. The guys really like it. I think they're good enough to put on the menu."
>
> At that point, my dad was like, "What are you talking about? You belong in Hollywood! You're gonna reinvent French fries? I think it's ridiculous! That will never work."

Lucky for us, instead of following his advice, Pete went on to add those "other things" and invented the famous Chickie's & Pete's "Crab Fries" that are known and loved today. Pete shared with us that, unfortunately, his dad did not live to see "how many millions of pounds of potatoes a year we use and how many different states we're in and how many different venues we're in around the country. But imagination did make a French fry different."

Throughout our conversation with Pete, two words really stood out—"imagination" and "persistence"—in particular, by way of a story he told us about his school days.

He described himself as "the kid looking out the window." It was his curiosity and "what if" attitude that engaged his thinking, along with lessons of school and teachers who believed in him. Pete believes this is where the magic of learning resides:

> If you can incorporate what you learn in school and incorporate what is known through your own ideas and your imagination, that's how things happen. That's how things explode and create new ideas. For example, if everybody was happy with a phone with a cord, we never would have had cordless phones, and then the iPhone. Know what I mean?

We do! Likewise, to possess genuine persistence with one's passion is critical to the success of any project, and all that starts with owning a positive attitude. In Pete's own words, "You have to have the determination and the fortitude to say, 'I'm going to stay with this! I believe in this! I think I can win! I can do it!' That's where success is!" Pete is so spot on with this point.

Like Stallone or Pete, those who are committed to a positive attitude, while establishing their individual values and behaviors, have a better chance of attaining their goals.

Imagine, for example, possessing a Rocky-like psyche as a caregiver (or educator), starting each morning with a driven desire to get to your place of employment, wanting to connect with the people, and maintaining that motivation throughout the day. Rocky had a champion attitude; losing was not in the cards—at least mentally. He refused to be defeated in the ring and in life. Stallone, as Rocky Balboa, reminds us, "Life's not about how hard of a hit you can give . . . it's about how many you can take, and still keep moving forward. That's how winning is done."[5]

The *Rocky* films are timeless in the sense that throughout the span of your life, a continuous provision of new stages and phases occur for you to approach as opportunities—opportunites to win: emotionally, physically, or mentally. The Rocky psyche is always applicable; it's always fitting if you want to move forward courageously. But, a crucial element that makes Rocky timeless is that opportunities are approached with the awareness that they will, some day, run out. Making progress matters. In reference to progress, Stallone, speaking as though he and his character were one in the same, has said, "I'm more focused and have a greater sense of challenge, because I constantly feel the weight of time."[6] Don't we all?

We know that "life is short"—we say it all the time in casual conversations. Yet we often forget to live it with a "GO!" attitude every day. Maybe we lack the discipline to stay focused. Focus, however, is something we don't have time to let wander. The gravity of time, of every moment, is perhaps most apparent when considering the challenge of connecting with the many different people we encounter every day.

You likely have only one, brief moment with any given person you encounter; therefore, your attitude must be ready to have a positive impact today—right now.

As Rocky Balboa's trainer, Mickey Goldmill, so eloquently said: "What are we waiting for?"

THE FOCUSED SELF: OWN YOUR ATTITUDE

Ask yourself what you are doing to embrace life every day. If you could gauge the temperature of your fire for living, what would it be? Look at the factors in your life that contribute to your positive attitude. When you have a powerful day with sustained energy, what was definitively different?

Start implementing changes into your daily life that are going to mold a positive mindset wherein you see life as full of possibility and every day as an opportunity for greatness. Respect that the *weight of time* is prevalent and constantly upon you. Your attitude is within your control and your ability to keep it engaged and positive will fuel your purpose and benefit those around you.

As Pete shared with us, we must "believe in ourselves and believe we can do it better. And if you can do it better, other people will eventually believe that, too." In other words, Pete is challenging us to adjust our attitude to focus on what we believe is possible and then to go and grab it full force! *Do something you love because then it's not work. Be great at it!* Be it in the French fry business or any work environment, our job as leaders is to equip our people with as many tools as possible so that, they too, can refine their attitudes and focus on their primary function with positive spirits and the kind of energy worth catching.

We both played on a basketball team when we were younger, and our coach used to voice to us that "there are only two things you can control, your attitude and your effort." Enough said.

NOTES

1. All Pete Ciarrocchi quotes presented in this chapter are from a phone interview with the authors that took place on May 10, 2018.
2. Rocky Balboa (played by actor Sylvester Stallone) is the lead fictional character of the iconic American film series *Rocky* (8 films in total, the first of which was released in 1976.
3. Sylvester Stallone, "Sylvester Stallone Quotes," *Brainy Quotes* (website): www.brainyquote.com.
4. Ibid.
5. Sylvester Stallone (Rocky Balboa), "Quotes," *goodreads* (website): www.goodreads.com.
6. Sylvester Stallone, "Quotes," *Brainy Quotes* (website): www.brainyquote.com.

Part II
AN OUTWARD JOURNEY OF THE HEART

Now that we have thought about some of the critical pieces to maximizing our self-worth within the framework of leadership and life, we can begin to magnify who we are, making our relationships and our teams tremendous.

When folks talk about the word "heart" in reference to work, they think of whole-heartedness, or complete effort. Although the activities associated with daily work are important (grading papers, making sandwiches, selling cars, etc.), we want to focus upon both the way life is an extension of ourselves and what lies concealed to the unnoticing eyes—relationships. Here, and only here, can we activate our hearts in order to become open to the possibility of making a greater impact beyond ourselves! In simple terms, only through the mind and heart may the hands eventually extend.

8

Put in a Contributing Piece to Someone Else's Puzzle

Trust the Process

> Trust the process through the eyes of a teacher.
>
> —Angelo R. Perryman, *president and CEO, Perryman Construction*[1]

Ironically, the adage *Trust the Process* has taken pop culture by storm. Not only was it evident as a chant at a recent NBA game, but T-shirts and sweatshirts advertise and promote it. We are hard-pressed to find a more fitting profession than education that best exemplifies the adage.

Sam Hinkie, former Philadelphia 76ers NBA General Manager from 2013 to 2016, approached his leadership role with a patient attitude to rebuild a losing, dare we say desperate, team. To gain top picks in the draft, Hinkie, and the Philadelphia players, endured three years of losses and setbacks—part of Hinkie's master plan known as *the process*. Ultimately, Hinkie wanted fans and league supporters to *trust the process* (and his intentions) to establish a winning team of players. Joel Embiid, a 2014 first-round draft pick from the University of Kansas, embraced the phrase and serves as a product of the plan and is representative of the adage. In fact, home game Philly fans have been heard chanting *Trust the Process* when Embiid approaches the free throw line. With Embiid, the legacy of Hinkie's dismal era survives in Philadelphia and is evidence that a patient approach avails.

Similarly, our role in the classroom (or yours in the workforce) is a genuine *Trust the Process* approach to building lives and influencing people. It is your hope that every child, every employee, becomes a successful, Joel Embiid, kind of story. Your impressions are powerful, yet the outcome of your actions can go unascertained every day. Much like the gloomy, vacant years of the 76ers, some days can feel winless, like you are in a battleground that will not produce heroes, winners, or even survivors.

However, the classroom (be it in a school setting or workplace) provides a platform for us to impart knowledge, character, and passion in a relational format, and we do this by building a plan and trusting in its outcomes.

For example, just as Joel did not blossom right out of college, there are also students and employees that may take time to grow into the superstar we first thought they would be. Angelo Perryman, of Perryman Construction, believes in this mantra when it comes to schools and the workplace. In his words, Angelo believes that "somewhere in the process, you had to believe that the system that was setup, to trust that the system was really going to deliver what was promised."

Although referencing our current educational system, we believe that Angelo's words manifest themselves into a broader context. One of the most critical mistakes we can make as leaders is rushing. We have all heard of the old adage "Haste makes waste," but it is never so true in education. Too often, teachers try to "cram the curriculum" into our students without truly assessing if they have learned the material or not. Of course, we are not blaming teachers here. We understand the pressures that come with high-stakes testing and the necessity to cover material.

However, somewhere along the line, we (as a nation) have forgotten the initial intent of education itself—that is, to assist our students to think and reason, to be problem solvers and to become socially aware of themselves and others. We are not trying to make a political statement, only to simply state that speed does not often result in a true grasp of thinking.

Likewise, we have to allow our students and employees to work together in order to build trust within themselves and for the mission and vision of the company. Angelo told us an amazing story about this concept through his days of coaching his kids:

> When my kids were younger, I used to coach soccer, but soccer was not a big sport where I grew up in the southeast. Baseball and football were that way. And the number one thing, I bet you if I said it once, I said it 400 times to a group of eight-year-olds is 'Stop Bunching.' (Around here, we call it bee ball—basically, the young athletes are like bees all flying around the hive—the soccer ball.)
>
> And somewhere in there, you have to get them to believe that somebody else has that space on the field covered. And it's hard for people to believe it, but once you get them to accept the concept that you can trust another person, who you don't know, who you may have preconceived ideas about, who you may have fault with the day before, but now you're teammates. . . . Once you get them to understand that they are going to cover their territory while you cover your territory, then you can get people to work together. We use that basic philosophy throughout our process (at Perryman).

As educators, we trust the process of our interactions every day. We sometimes do not see the fruits of our labors come to be, especially if we teach younger students. In other words, although every year there is a graduating class, not every teacher in the district gets to experience that day. No. Our successes, our smaller and each step of the way contribute to the whole. Therefore, we must cherish the moments and interactions we have with our students each and every day.

We would venture to state that Angelo bases his company's success on the work. In simple terms, the process of getting folks to collaborate ultimately yields high-quality opportunities and relationships for folks, which, in turn, creates high yields for the company. In his words, "I always like to treat people the way I wanted to be treated. It is a safe place. Confidence will allow you to go deeper into a person than most would. And, some of that is knowing that you can handle a situation once you're there."

Makes perfect sense. Have you ever met a person that is just so negative to her daily routine? Most times, when we root to the core of their misery, there is a belief that this person was "wronged or underappreciated" by their students, colleagues, or clients. In order to be truly effective in building relationships, we cannot build them for the chance to "get something out of it." For example, we don't teach every day for the confirmation that we are successful; we do it every day because we trust the process that students will someday benefit from our influence. Similar to Hinkie, we foresee a victorious ending to the story and *that* drives our passion and actions. Students benefit from teachers who are *going for the win*. Teachers see the potential in students, trusting that the persistent, daily, patient attitude will avail and be advantageous for the student.

Similarly, Angelo states that "you've got to be able to listen to what it is they want to be. And if there's something you can do, do it." Being able to deliver on our relationship promises is key in establishing lasting trust. The reality is that we would be underchallenged if all of our students came to school motivated, interested, and dedicated. Think about it, imagine your students conforming to rules and order and wanting to perform above and beyond expectations. The employment line for educator job placement would be lengthy!

We do experience students in our careers who exemplify these traits and make us want to teach to truly make a difference. "Trust the process" is more applicable to the students who are just the opposite. Students who come to school unmotivated, disinterested, and apathetic are challenging to invest in, and our lens for their future is blurred and uncertain. We might even say those types of students erode us throughout the year. **But when we teach with the patient attitude that every child has a story, a purpose, and a future, and when we *trust the process* that coincides with that attitude, we impart power in the classroom.**

Be it school or construction, the process to completion is something that Angelo values dearly. "And probably that's what I like about it (referencing construction and his company), that you're always building, you're building the people, you're building the projects, you're building a different type of understanding for owners, you're building relationships. It's a constant building process. And somewhere in between all those intersections is somebody that succeeds at all different levels." We, too, see the parallel and can acknowledge that although it may feel like the educational world is made up of sub-contractors, the end result is a flexible mind ready to be lived in and changed as our experiences (and trust) grow.

THE FOCUSED HEART: OWN THE PROCESS

As Angelo stated numerous times, in the process, you have to believe that the system is set up with trust. Too often, we allow ourselves to succumb to the negativity of our work is never done. Our strength lies in our ability to have faith in students and in their unique purpose. When we build relationships with our students, be confident that all the interactions, positive and negative, are part of the developmental process for the end result (which you may never witness or experience).

Be invigorated by the fact that you trust the unknown. Think about how powerful that is! The outcome of your investment every day is mysterious, often an enigma. As long as we continue to have the confidence that we are making a difference, we will continue to have the desire to go back, day after day. We plant seeds every day with students—not knowing the progress or growth that lies ahead. Be open minded to what is transpiring with a student and persevere relationally even if it challenges us.

It is also worth mentioning again that students (and staff) can develop at different times. Angelo emphasized, "For us, our story builds upon giving people a chance." It parallels with the belief that kids open up their gifts at different times. Over time, you have to look at their heart, sometimes overlooking their actions.

NOTE

1. All Angelo R. Perryman quotes presented in this chapter are from an in-person interview with the authors that took place on May 22, 2018.

9

Put on Your Glasses and Really SEE the Person!

Cultivate Strengths

> I think you hit the nail on the head with coping strategies. Also, who is taking the time to do the character development with people, particularly when we start talking about grit? How do we help kids (and others) identify their grit and how to deal with these obstacles?
>
> —Marcus Allen, *CEO,*
> *Big Brothers Big Sisters Independence Region*[1]

Marcus Allen is the CEO of Big Brothers Big Sisters Independence. Influential, passionate, and genuinely caring, he operates an organization that strives to instill hope in our young people by providing supports necessary for success. To say that this is a necessary job, we can think of no other task in the entire world more critical than assisting our youth to become successful adults. But prior to students becoming successful adults, they must first be successful children and teenagers. And many times, that success is predicated on an environment that allows kids to fail forward and learn from their mistakes. That process must be met with understanding, love, and care.

One of the most powerful stories we had heard through this entire journey was related to us by Marcus and his experience with Linda Cliatt-Wayman:

> A friend of mine, Linda Cliatt-Wayman, has a tremendous lesson for all of us when it comes to instilling hope and strength in our youth. Strawberry Mansion was known as one of the most violent and dangerous schools in America. When Linda was there, she used to be more of an administrator at the central office, and she was trying to find someone to run the school yet no one would take the job of principal for Strawberry Mansion High School. The school was known for having 96 percent of their students living in poverty, 10 violent incidents per 100 students and teachers were constantly being assaulted. The school had gone through 4 principals in 4 years.

One day, Linda said she was walking into her office and this voice inside her said, "Stop looking; you already have the person!" At that, she went into central office, and she told the superintendent that she wanted to run that school.

Linda took a demotion to go and run that school. And one of the things she told me sticks with me to this day.

"Marcus—Many of our kids don't hear I love you. Do you hear me? Many of our kids don't hear I love you."

So every morning, even if the kids called it whack, or whatever slang term kids use, every morning, she would start out on the intercom and say if nobody told you that they loved you today, then I'm telling you right now, I love you.

And not only would she tell the kids that she loved them but she would show them that she loved in the way that she dealt with them, even when there were fights that broke out, she would get right in the middle of the fights. When there were kids that were being bullied, she would say, "okay show me the kid that is bullying you; let's have a conversation and the three of us are going to sit down and figure this out."

When the kids had issues at home or in the streets, she was there; she would make sure that she and her teachers were there talking to these kids. Where Strawberry Mansion is located, there's a lot of crime in that area, so for the first day of school, she would have the teachers walk the students home.

The kids respond, whether they let you know or not, they respond, and they knew teachers really cared about them. It went a long, long way.

By tough love, rigorous rules, and consequences, Linda's efforts at Strawberry Mansion High School produced results. After one year, the literature and algebra scores more than doubled, Diane Sawyer from ABC spent an entire year documenting Linda's efforts, celebrity rapper Drake gave a significant donation to start a music program at the school, they started their first football team that went undefeated in the first year, test scores improved every year, and the school was removed from the federal Persistently Dangerous Schools list for the first time in five years.

In a utopic classroom or work community, we know the strengths of each of our students/employees; likewise, we guide those strengths so that people excel not only in their work but also in their lives. Utopic environments are filled with motivated folks who are happy to be utilizing their best traits for a greater purpose. The challenge we face is Shangri-La, which rarely presents itself in a class or corporate room.

Recognizing the challenges teachers face, Marcus encourages that despite necessary tools and resources,

> At a minimum, I can make these kids feel good about where they are, who they are and let them know that there's someone who cares about them. For me, I think the rest of it will take care of itself. If you're a trained teacher, you know how to teach kids, you know how to move them along some spectrum of learning, right? If you underlay that with a foundation of: **I don't know everything that you're dealing with, *but I see you*, you show up to me as someone who has just as much potential as any other person, any other student I've taught. I think that says a lot to a kid.**

All of us have strengths, but seeing those strengths takes a different lens. All of us bring value to a given situation; but rarely as human beings, do we take the time to learn about someone else's value. One strategy that Marcus has at his core is how he *shows up* every day. He reminds us that it is not about how others show up but how you show up. That type of perspective has a direct impact and as a CEO, he assured us, "They didn't hire me to come in and manage great employees, they hired me to come in and help those employees who needed help to get to their greatness." **When you show up in a way that opens up your heart for others, you can elevate others simply by potentiating their skills and abilities.**

Marcus's approach reflects the importance of vulnerability. "It's always important to be vulnerable to kids because kids can see when you are not authentic." Sometimes, in our vulnerability, we suppress the need to talk and the need to listen reigns supreme. It is in this moment where we get to know people, especially kids.

As we were chatting with Marcus, he emphasized that getting to know kids through providing them with guidance and direction is not enough, but the conversation has to put the end in mind for the listener; in other words, I don't want you just to get there or get better just to check off the box, I want to make sure you know *how* to get there! "So what that says to me when we think about our kids is that everyone enters the classroom fearful, we have to help (embrace this fear). Many times, as adults, we talk to kids and say, 'you gotta get over this, you gotta do better at this;' but, we don't talk to them about *how to do it*, we talk to them about the goal, about what we need them to do, but we don't walk them through step by step what that looks like."

An example of this insecurity can manifest itself in a visit to the local home improvement store. There are many times that we visit these places of enormous choice only to feel insecure about a project we have never prior attempted, let alone accomplished. As the time in the aisle lapses, our brains race with fear. All the while, we hope that some "nice" person will give us the courtesy of assistance and, at the same time, won't think of us as "dumb."

Be it in the classroom or in the store aisle, discovering inherent motivations and strengths stems from genuine interaction and a personal desire to get to know someone and their needs.

Critical to this charge is the challenge to honor people who are different than us. There is great simplicity in connecting with and getting to know people (especially, our students) with whom we share similar traits. For example, our highly organized, enthusiastic attitude with a keen eye for detail synchronizes well with a top-notch student Sally who crosses every T, dots every I, comes prepared, and sits eagerly in the front row of your classroom.

Conversely, challenging are the students who are *not* like us, and, more so, possess traits that we do not respect or honor: disorganized or even disengaged. We struggle to understand what motivates them. For instance, please consider this scenario:

While other students, such as our previously mentioned Sally, are boasting about the enjoyment of the floating egg lab in science class, Eddie exemplifies rebellious behaviors. He spends several minutes looking for a pencil, then he asks to go to the bathroom, and, ultimately, he begins disruptively spinning the egg on the table like a top. In the midst of that scene, if you were advised to honor Eddie's persona and make a positive connection with him, you might have a hard time doing so.

Herein resides the challenge. Teachers are expected to get to know all students—students whom we might not otherwise care to know and students who, quite honestly, frustrate us. To enhance the lives of all students, we need to hold ourselves accountable as their teacher; we need to get to know them to honor their value and worth. To that end, we must first believe each student *has* value and worth. Sometimes that original premise is the most difficult.

As Marcus so beautifully put it, "Students don't expect us to solve everything because they know we're all flawed, right? They know we are not half as smart as we try to put on. They know that, but (what they want to see is) we will put in the effort. And that's what matters to them just like it would matter to any adult."

When we think back to that trip to the lumber yard, Marcus's words ring so true. **What people desire from us is an earnest effort!** People desire those in service to eagerly adopt the honorable mindset that every person has worth. Whether I know a two by four from a four by six, I am here. I want to try and learn. And I need you to help me. Even if I do not know the exactness of the task, honor my strength of adventure and my spirit to try to accomplish something that causes me to doubt myself and my ability.

For teachers, every student in our classroom will become an adult and will further become an integral part of society. Our classroom is a microcosm of society, and to disregard any personality as not as worthy or as important as another is to diminish the effectiveness and interconnectedness of a society.

Likewise, we may never become a master carpenter, but perhaps, just perhaps, we will have enough confidence to build that picnic table for our families to enjoy dinner together under the star-lit sky. And when we do, perhaps I will remember the person who took some time to help me build my skill set to make this dream happen.

Recognizing value through seeking out strengths is an optimal way of building a desirable classroom and a desirable work environment. It is not our place to discern which person is more valuable than another, much like it is not our place to get to know one person better than another. Reverting to Sally and Eddie, a soothsayer might predict that Sally's future is the role of a CEO, hypothetically Company X. Eddie's future, conversely, is the role of a server at Company X. Accurate or not, fast-forward the story as if it had validity to it: ask yourself this question, when you go out to lunch at Company X, who is more critical to the outcome of a delicious, hot, made to order lunch—the CEO or the server? Now go back and evaluate your attitude toward Sally and Eddie; it makes us question how we could possibly dismiss the value of Eddie.

Too often, human beings have a tendency to dismiss the negativity that we have grown accustomed to witnessing via the social media explosion. Marcus has heard it deemed, "The Philly Shrug—Oh well, sorry I can't do anything to help you. I care, but I don't care that much."

But, as Marcus encourages, "We have to remind ourselves that some of this is simple, whether we created it or not, we have a responsibility to at least try to do our part to correct it."

The significance of getting to know students and customers, while cultivating their strengths, arises from your own ability to see every individual as integral and esteemed. Bringing a persona to the classroom or showroom that is secure, focused, and unburdened, as mentioned in the Inward Journey of the Self section of this text, is our initial critical role.

Every interaction matters and can make a difference in building up a person. Become aware of what students do well, what comes easy to them, what makes them feel good about themselves, what others positively say about them, and what their dreams are. Knowing these basic strengths is a foundation you can build on; it also provides a platform for you to encourage connectedness among similar students. When we gauge these strengths, there is greater potential for cultivating a person who sees himself as purposeful, valued, loved, and accepted.

With positive self-perceptions, people will gain a greater sense of authenticity, self-actualization, and a passion for life that will ignite their hearts and maintain an ascending trajectory through their next dinner under the stars or through life itself.

THE FOCUSED HEART: OWN A CULTIVATING SPIRIT

Momentarily, shift your focus to society. Write down or make mental notes of all the people you interact with or who fulfill a need for you in a day. Your list might contain: a mail delivery person, a trash collector, a coffee shop employee, a police officer, a principal, a teacher, an athletic coach, a parent, a doctor, a waitress, a manager, and so on. Picture these individuals as students in your classes—what descriptors do you assign? Studious, organized, average, above average, disheveled, punctual, neat, and so on.

As you teach your classes or serve your client, do you make the mistake of valuing people *less* because you struggle to find their strengths? Do you value people *more* because you seamlessly find their strengths? Is that fair?

The people who are *perceived* as doing menial, basic jobs in society are usually the people who we would miss the most if they stopped working. For many, we would be willing to bet that the coffee shop employee not showing up to serve coffee just might be catastrophic.

Students matter. People matter. We all matter!

So, be mindful of how you perceive them. Connect with people, discover, and cultivate their gifts—that's what it means to be an educator, be it in the classroom or in corporate.

Lastly, we would like to end this chapter with a short anecdote from Marcus that we hope you will incorporate (even in theory) into your daily dealing with human beings:

I used to do work on the Native American reservations, and one of the things that really stuck with me from the Crow Indian nation in Billings Montana was their ceremonies, symbols and rituals that were passed down through word of mouth. Their custom was that they did not write things down; neither did their ancestors, and they have been doing this for hundreds of years.

The organization I worked for borrowed some of their ceremonies and symbols and rituals to implement those in our work with kids. We had a practice called a circle and anytime we met, we would meet in a circle. There's four directions on the circle, north, south, east and west, and each pole on the circle meant something. I would stand in the north, which is a place of leadership, and someone would stand in the east, which is the place of touch, someone would reside in the south the place of commitment, and someone would stay in the west the place of control (your environment, self-control, financial control, etc.).

We had to come into the circle in silence, and then the person standing in the North Pole would say, "What goes around comes around." Then, he or she would turn to the person to their right, give them a hug, little heart to heart, my heart on your heart and every one of those kids did that all the way around the circle until the hug gets back to the person in the North. Now the circle's complete.

The key here is to understand and respect all the positions, to not see any position as less or more important but to see all as critical to the circle's complete circumference. When we can see every individual as purposeful, it is a complete perspective. We all stand on different circles in our personal life as well as in our professional life. If we view those circles as two-dimensional objects, it is important that as we look across our circles we see people who stand on the same imaginary plane as we do; no one is higher or lower than anyone on the circle. Yet, all of us have different perspectives depending upon where we stand on the circle. Let's reinforce the idea that no one is more or less valuable; we all matter.

NOTE

1. All Marcus Allen quotes presented in this chapter are from an in-person interview with the authors that took place on May 15, 2018.

10

Seeing Problems? You Might Need New Glasses!

View Challenges as Opportunities

> I'm looking for progress in myself and the people around me. Challenges spur us to do our best and help us find happiness in work and in life. Knowing how not to do something often brings us one step closer to knowing the right way.
>
> —Bernard Dagenais, *president and CEO, The Main Line Chamber of Commerce*[1]

Aside from being a highly successful CEO of The Main Line Chamber of Commerce, Bernard Dagenais is a wonderful example of grit factor; his personal and professional story mirrors the essence of perseverance. One such instance simply had to be included in this text:

> I was heading into my junior year of college when I flunked Newswriting. My class adviser informed me it was time to change my major from journalism to something else because I clearly didn't belong in the program and had no business becoming a journalist.
>
> The major problem with his advice was that, only weeks before as part of the same class, I had been assigned to ride a public bus, talk to people and to find and write a story based on one of those interviews.
>
> At 20 years old, I was suddenly hooked on the idea of having the license to talk to pretty much anyone about pretty much anything.
>
> So I took extra courses in the summer and recommitted to getting through the program, leading to a bachelor of arts of journalism followed by a 27-year career as an award-winning reporter and editor. My work appeared in newspapers, on websites, and on television and radio.
>
> It was a fulfilling job that brought me from small-town school board meetings in Vermont to the White House and the halls of Congress. The communications skills I developed, first as a writer and later as a manager, public speaker and regular interviewee on television news, formed the basis of my current career as president and CEO of a regional Chamber of Commerce that works each day to help our member companies succeed.

Looking back, that confrontation with the class adviser was a pivotal moment. Of course I'm not proud of getting an F in my core subject, but my reaction to it helped make me who I am today—someone who doesn't quit when it matters.

There were other examples in which I learned from challenges, like working for a difficult boss, moving to a new part of the country where I knew no one as a high school senior and my accelerated recovery from a life-threatening car accident in more recent years.

These are the times when you take stock of yourself and your life. I wasn't OK with failing out of the journalism program. I decided I would not be a boss who rules from a place of fear. I realized that life was too short to not address issues that stood in the way of my happiness. **I've learned that my experience isn't so different from many others who are shaped by the challenges they face.**

We pretty much could end the chapter right there (but we won't). As we stated, Bernie's tales were too profound to allow just one to manifest.

Procrastination is king in some folks. The old adage "I'll get to it tomorrow," can overtake us in a world where seemingly everyone else has not only started the race before us but is way out in front. However, the issue of accountability arises when closure is disregarded and an opportunity is missed. Much like marital advice, such as "Don't go to bed angry," or parenting advice, such as "Always kiss your child goodnight," educator advice should be, "Circle back with care before the final bell rings."

Perhaps our inability to see challenges as opportunities lies within misperception. Did we start the day off with a *rough launch* that we allowed to become a runaway freight train? Maybe we blamed the challenges on the student because after all, *Frank is always that way*. Evaluating our heart's inward journey is a crucial step to striving for both teachable moments but attainable ones as well.

We must be open to genuine conversations with ourselves and others by focusing on building relationships, even though it can be challenging.

Life is not easy. Think about it. As Bernie reminded us:

It starts early. The first thing a baby does at birth is to fight for breath. A newborn's cry is always considered a good sign, as it shows the baby is breathing. Each of us is born struggling.

What happens to people who embrace the struggle of life into adulthood? For one thing, they succeed in ways that others don't. They adapt and learn, for example, how to juggle the complexities of a busy life. They decide that, whatever their shortcomings or disadvantages, there's value in doing the best they can. They understand they will make mistakes. They may be hard on themselves and that can be a good thing. They get past the errors and grow.

As someone who has for 30 years managed teams of people, with a goal of leading them to do their best and achieve important goals, I clearly explain to those who work for me that I don't ask for or expect perfection. There are more important things, like genuinely trying for example, which leads to improvement. I'm looking for progress, in myself and the people around me. Challenges spur us to do our best and help us find happiness in work and in life.

Of course, results matter. If a task has to be done 100 percent right, as in a life-and-death situation, safeguards are to be encouraged. In much of life, a mistake isn't such a big deal. An error might be more notable for the level of progress it brings than how much it sets things back. Knowing how not to do something often brings us one step closer to knowing the right way.

If Bernie was a teacher in a classroom, there is no doubt that he would agree that students forgetting homework, running in the halls, being unkind to other students, not telling the truth, being disruptive, cheating on a test, and so on, are all examples of mistakes and challenges. But Bernie would also see those events as opportunities to engage with students. They are seizable moments where we can teach students that mistakes are necessary; how will we learn what is proper if we never receive guidance about what is improper? To have progress, there must be growth! Mistakes and challenges feed our growth.

Bernie's words on failure secure this point when it comes to students or staff alike:

F.A.I.L. is only an acronym for First Attempt in Learning, as one colleague puts it. It's a theme in many successful careers. In history, there's Thomas Edison who made 1,000 attempts to invent the light bulb before he got it right. As an employee and student, he appeared to fit the classic definition of "a loser," a term that should clearly be rethought. Wisdom can be found in fiction as well as in history. In one of the Batman movies, a young Bruce Wayne is asked why someone falls. The answer, his butler/companion Alfred says, is: "so we can learn to pick ourselves up."

It's reasonable to think that the same error should not be repeated, but allowances can be made because people learn differently from each other. Patience is a powerful tool in so many things, including teaching. How one responds to a mistake either creates an opportunity to learn or causes those who err to simply stop trying.

The intolerable offense for an employee, in my book, is to not care.

Every manager is faced with a decision when working with an employee who doesn't understand how to accomplish a task. Do you do it yourself or take the time to teach the person? While doing the project yourself might be more efficient at first, in the long run, it will take longer while an opportunity to learn and grow is missed.

The most admirable leaders don't just focus on achieving goals, such as making more money for example. Rather, they help those around them to grow. This can lead to uncomfortable moments when a message must be delivered that standards aren't being met. That's where authenticity comes into the equation. If you can help people to understand that you care about them, they will be more receptive to your guidance. If you can help them to understand the value of receiving feedback in a non-defensive way, you help them along a path to success. It often helps to give them a glimpse of how you are working to improve yourself.

In any endeavor, having the right people around you makes goals more achievable. Rarely, however, do employees start a job knowing what to do and how to do it. They will face challenges and if you help them through those challenges, you are rewarded by witnessing their growth and, perhaps even, winning their appreciation.

Holding ourselves accountable in subsequent attempts is just as important as the first attempt.

Chapter 10

THE FOCUSED HEART:
OWN THE VISION; ASSIST OTHERS IN THEIRS

In a chapter about having grit (or heart), you did not think we would not include the most infamous hearts of all time—The Grinch, did you? (Remember, we are teachers. We love to add stories like this to prove our points.)

Picture the scene in *How the Grinch Stole Christmas* where the Grinch, who once had the dark heart of a thief, followed by Max, his faithful but gloomy dog, is struggling to save the overloaded sleigh of presents from escaping down the mountainside. In the scene, the Grinch suddenly has a transformation, *What happened then? Well, in Whoville they say—that the Grinch's small heart grew three sizes that day.* And with his heart not so tight, his generous spirit grew.

Whereas the Grinch once delighted in hoarding all of the gifts to himself, he soon recognized his transgression and had a change of heart. The once heavy, cumbersome sleigh would soon be unburdened for Max the dog and the gifts would bring smiles to the faces of the Whos in Whoville. We should make it our personal Grinch goal to own our own mistakes and ensure all people (especially students) leave us with a heart two or three sizes bigger. Doing so empowers their confidence for success and our own hearts just might grow in tandem! In education we call this "circling back."

Circling back is a tactic we use to ensure that everyone is grasping the concept. The practice, however, is not giving out answers to students. It's simply providing time and support for those engaged in the struggle of a challenge. Perhaps an encouraging word or even a little mental nudge can sometimes be all it takes to set the mind and heart sailing.

In the last words from Bernie, "It's up to us as teachers and managers to show what it means to learn and to care, while finding those teachable moments. Embracing challenges, as opportunity rather than weakness, is quite simply the path to a better life."

NOTE

1. All Bernard Dagenais quotes presented in this chapter are from a written contribution provided May 22, 2018; emphasis added.

11

Engaging with People Can Actually Be Fun? Yes It Can!

Invest in Relationships

> People do not work for Wawa to make hoagies, serve coffee and run registers. They work here to try and make their friends' and neighbors' days better. And when we serve people like that, it's of the highest purpose and one of the noblest pursuits we can have.
>
> —Chris Gheysens, *president and CEO, Wawa, Inc.*[1]

Our friends who are financial analysts loved the title of this chapter. In fact, their entire livelihood is dependent upon it. As a matter of course, they make money when we allow them to invest ours. Quite an enigma—if we "save" money for retirement, they "spend" it in order to produce both more savings and their own salary. Sure, they call it investing, but truth be told, they are spending it on stocks or bonds; whereas we would have spent it on a new car or wardrobe.

When we were first starting out in our jobs, both of us invested our money with financial representatives not necessarily because we totally understood everything about mutual funds and 403Bs, but because of the way we were treated by these individuals, and the patience they took in developing a plan for us. Their behaviors were impressive, consistently checking in to make sure we were okay with what they were doing, giving us up-to-date feedback on our investments, and suggesting changes when needed.

Needless to say, these men and women were financially literate and quite capable in their professional skill set, but more important than those economic skills, they were extremely adept in human being proficiencies. Think about it: *It's not easy to hand strangers your money!* Therefore, to attain our business, they had to develop a relationship with us, so that we would not only know them, but also trust them enough to turn over our hard-earned cash.

While working on this book, it was not uncommon for us to grow weary at times. After all, our full-time jobs and our families take up a great deal of time and energy.

One afternoon, we were thinking about a good spot to grab a cup of coffee, and Joy immediately suggested, "Let's run out to my Wawa."

When we thought about this chapter, and the importance of investing in the relationships of our students, employees, and customers, we both immediately reminisced about the day we went to "Joy's Wawa."

Obviously, Joy does not own the Wawa, but she does identify the motto of "My," which was one of the most ingenious marketing ads in our area. The cool idea about this campaign is that it's not a campaign. It's a way of doing business. You see, "My Wawa" evokes the notion of family, and that is exactly what Chris Gheysens, CEO of Wawa, Inc., wants us to not only think of, but feel.

Chris is very passionate about the importance of culture and purpose at Wawa and how both drive strong relationships and family-like bonds with customers: "Customer relationship business is the most powerful way of creating a culture and then rewarding those people with ownership and a voice in the process. There are so many elements of (building a successful business), but they are the primary ones."

During our conversation, Chris talked much about building a mission and vision for the purpose of business. In simple terms, Chris sees the experiences at Wawa as an opportunity to expand social relationships. This experience then can transcend products, which, in turn, drives success (recall our financial investor—we have to spend to save).

Chris describes Wawa as a "people first, high engagement, high touch culture." Through hiring the right people and establishing an environment and culture of care, opportunities are created where people "can really go above and beyond and make somebody's day amazing," and countless stories in the retail stores are evidence of that happening daily at Wawa!

As educators, we often say that before we can invest in instructional strategies that work with students, we must first invest in them as people. Maya Angelou succinctly put it this way: "I've learned that people will forget what you said, people will forget what you did, but people will never forget how you made them feel."[2]

Investing in kids for who they are, not for how they perform or what materials they bring every day, constructs a meaningful partnership with limitless benefits. In order to realize this task, we must be able to recognize the power of instruction without disregard for the importance of relational construction.

Construct relationships with students and families that are intentional and purpose driven.

If this concept resonates in schools, why would it not resound in business? In life?

It takes sharp discipline to separate *who* a person is from *how* he or she acts in a given situation. We, unfortunately, carry layers of bias to our classrooms and conference rooms without malicious intention. It is here, within the concept of "my," that the heart of "our" lives. In other words, if this is both my Wawa *and* your Wawa, then ultimately it is ours.

The best of teachers use this type of language with students. They structure classroom procedures with a collaborative spirit; they establish social norms with cooperation in mind, and they almost certainly refer to the space as "our" classroom.

Within the business of doing business, we must reevaluate our initial perceptions and work hard to adopt an *investment mindset*, whereby the more we put into others, the greater our return.

Chris refers to this concept as "unexpected care." He stated that "this idea of unexpected care is sort of a manifestation of our best moments, our perfect moments, of when our culture is great. A (positive) culture takes investment and nurturing, and if culture is about building relationships, it's not just the end relationship with customer (that counts). It means, 'How do I build relationships with our associates? How does every leader build relationships? How do we empower people and serve people?' (Each day,) we talk about servant leadership, and we lead a servant leadership model here."

What we understood of this concept is what we witness when we visit our local Wawa store. The people that work there are not just folks but friends. They say, "Hello." They get to know your name and do the "little things" that go a long way into the decision to revisit the store again, and again, and again. And this type of core value must start at the top.

Be it a teacher or the CEO of Wawa, "We learn over time, if our job as a leader is to serve and engage versus command and control, we then flip the paradigm! My job here is one to set up an atmosphere of respect in our environment."

Of course, this mindset does not just solely work with the corporate world but in education as well. Our colleagues should also be afforded the opportunity to be known. Sure, there will be some who choose to keep to themselves, and that is their decision to make. Yet, we know folks in our schools who have worked together for thirty years and have never ever had a meaningful conversation with one another.

As we were gathering our qualitative research, we chatted with a few of these folks. Their rationales were simple—we are in different departments; we are not on the same floor; we have always had different lunch periods. The justifications went on and on. Truly, think about people who have worked together for three decades never to have really talked with one another. Pretty eye opening!

One of the theoretical themes that emerged from the interviews was that these folks, although in the same district and building (some even in the same department), did not see themselves as "in this together." They were nice enough people, but they exuded the "lone wolf" mentality. Thus, the need for connection from everyone was not existent. In other words, they were either content on being alone or they had their people, and, if you were not one of them, it was not personal.

Now, think back to students or customers again. The lack of that personal connection causes the kink in the chain that ultimately causes the disconnection in one's educational or consumer journey.

In simple terms, the breakdown is revealed in a student struggling to solve a math problem, but the real struggle is underneath the surface of the math. Without a genuine relationship, we look to fix the alleged math incompetency issue, missing the mark in the emotional realm. A simple "Are you okay today?" constructs a meaningful relationship versus "Do you need to review the chapter?" which merely addresses mastery of content.

Investing in people is nothing new; it is a timeless practice that must be returned into our conscience often. As Chris states, "Leaders need to figure out what makes each person tick and what motivates them to engage. We must not come at this from a position of power (do what I say). We are at the same level."

According to Chris, "It's gotta be like this, intertwined, it's really a people first strategy, it's *here's how we invest in people, we care about them and we develop and invest in them personally*, so not to oversimplify it but it does boil down to culture and leadership."

Supporting the people-first strategy, Chris shared an anecdote about Miss Harriet.

> So, when we introduced coffee pots, and we have these big urns now and I go and speak to Miss Harriet, who is ninety years old, who, when you came in, she would hug you, and she said I can't lift the urn, it's too heavy, I can't do this anymore. Oh my gosh! We didn't think about it, we felt like we talked to every customer in the world, you know, taste this, is this good? For a year! But never went to Miss Harriet and asked, so all of a sudden, I thought, wow, it's a big problem so she would just stand there and wipe down the coffee island.

We must assimilate this type of thinking to build relational wealth with everyone we meet.

THE FOCUSED HEART: OWN THE INVESTMENT

Start small. Take time and build relationships that will sustain. A simple smile or good morning at the door goes a long, long way in making students feel welcome and safe. Likewise, the same goes for adults. Initiate conversations and show a genuine interest; ask how their families are doing. Remember, we all have a life outside of our four walls.

Social conditioning of human beings is not a foreign concept. When we spend the majority of our adult lives at work, we sometimes become immune to new opportunities for investing. Here, unfortunately the familiar can become the mundane. In addition, the "same thing again" can start to become a burden. Here is where the complaining sets in. Do your best to break this cycle of habit with this simple maxim: **One of the smartest ways to build a positive relationship is to stay positive.** Those that develop a reputation of being complainers usually end up being alone and then they find someone to complain to about it.

With a growth mindset, you can see that change is possible in intelligence and personality. Your aptitude in feverishly attacking the notion that *it is what it is* must be substituted with *it is what it is—for now*. If a teacher has had an issue with a student, it does not mean that you will or vice versa. Therefore, build capacity to see each situation as new and inviting. Who knows, you just might find a hidden gem in a stock that you did not even know existed.

Chris describes the joy of Wawa and the joy of living with this powerful description:

> You can never underestimate a smile, a look in the eye, a thank you, a how are you doing? And it's easy and when those opportunities or windows present themselves, jump right through. And worst case, you get no response but maybe they smiled when they got in the car. Another customer may have seen that and had a reaction that was positive for them. And that one person goes and spreads that to someone else. Think about the impact you could have on your hometown and your community even with small caring gestures. That is our purpose, to fulfill lives, and make the communities that we serve more vibrant, better, and not just in the store, but what we do outside the store as well, by investing in communities.

NOTES

1. All Chris Gheysens quotes presented in this chapter are from an in-person interview with the authors that took place on May 4, 2018.
2. Maya Angelou, "Maya Angelou Quotes," *goodreads* (website): www.goodreads.com.

12

Labels Are Just for Soup Cans

Define Hearts, Despite Actions

> We can only change one behavior in life, and that is our own.
>
> —Denis P. O'Brien, *senior executive VP, advisor to CEO, Exelon Corporation*[1]

Sadly, in the educational field, sometimes children are labeled by their past actions. Too often, we hear of a student's trials from another teacher as a warning for the misery that is to come with having him or her in class. Quotes like, "You have Jerry next year? Look out!" can critically endanger the reputation and potential for success of a child. In addition, these so-called cautions can also infiltrate our own thinking when it comes to the person at hand, creating bias and a false sense of reality (Jerry is not a nice person) for that child.

We witness this pattern in society, too. A person makes a mistake, and he or she is ostracized from the masses as a person we should avoid. Of course, there are terrible acts that have every right to define a person, and, thus, people have to be responsible for their actions. But for the purpose of this chapter, we are not referring to major transgressions.

In being human beings, none of us are perfect. Built upon insecurity and imperfection, we sometimes try to categorize a person based upon a specific "box" in which he or she fits. These boxes can take on labels of race or gender or actions, yet make no mistake, they are all forms of biased behavior that can create a false narrative about a given human being and his or her story.

When speaking of this topic, Denis O'Brien, Sr. Executive VP and Advisor to CEO Exelon Corporation, was amazing at defining usable strategies for people to assist us in this arena. Denis stated that "I have learned to live with ambiguity; life's a good teacher for us, and we have to learn to live in ambiguity much longer and have much more patience with it."

This idea of ambiguity has much to do with our brain's desire to connect. As mentioned, the brain very much wants to "know" a situation by connecting previous thoughts to new ones. This "new" knowledge tends to cause us (even instantaneously) moments of insecurity, as our brains struggle to make sense of the data constantly coming at us. Hence, we have to fight the urge to "control" the thought prior to defining where it should reside in our minds.

Denis's experience has proven that "pushing us out of our comfort zone" helps us become more accepting of uncertainty. In thinking through this concept, Denis shared a tremendous approach to utilize when placed into "new" situations with people:

> When I would attend an event, they would ask if you want to come up and address the group. But since I like to be prepared when I meet people, (I would decline).
>
> (One time during an event, my friend saw me avoiding a particular group setting.) Sensing my uneasiness, my friend came up to me and said, "Denis, don't you know the 'act as if' theory? You act as if you love it, and eventually you will."
>
> Well, there's a lot of truth to this theory because now I love going into a group of people and working the room. But it took mental training in the "act as if you love" theory.
>
> When we act as if it (the event or idea) is the best thing we've ever done, it mimics behavioral science.
>
> Now, if I go through this building and pass by a meeting, I'll stop and say hi to everyone in the meeting; I'll ask them what are they are working on or tell them they did a great job with that, but it's all mentally trained. (It's a learned behavior.)

Similar to Denis's training with "act as if," our ability to see a person's heart past their actions is essential to stimulating growth. All too often, it is easy to dismiss people and the opportunities for genuine relationships with them because of something they did (or were rumored to have done). We need to remind ourselves that an action does not define a person. In other words, just because someone did something positive does not necessarily make him or her a good person. Conversely, if someone has made a mistake, it does not mean that he or she is wicked. **Being able to separate one's actions with one's persona is critical in cultivating sustainable relationships.**

Denis discussed his company and how he tries to instill a sense of personal connection with people in the hopes of breaking down the distance that too often can grow between people without communication and caring. As we do, Denis believes that "we have to look and say, 'What do I like about this person?' And we have to find it! Then, we need to focus on that (trait). If we can find that one point that we really like about a person and focus on it, that (allows for more opportunities and traits to like about him/her.) But not always easy."

We know! In schools, countless parent conferences are sounding boards for frustrated families, searching for answers to questions they have yet to discover about their child. These conversations can sometimes become passionate, and people can become upset with us or situations that are beyond our control.

In these tense moments, Denis's strategy of "finding one thing" can really work wonders. Our engaged listening, along with our ability to find the one common thread, can often be the difference between locating a solution or not.

In Denis's world, the job is literally "to keep the lights on." How many of us, during a power outage, have called our local company, had someone on the phone, and sadly let them have it for a situation that is no fault of theirs?

At Exelon, customer service agents are trained in active listening. They are skilled at being able to stay calm and truly digest the issues that people are facing in their daily lives. And even if they cannot fix the problem, they can and do provide caring service to their clients. Mainly because they do not see them as clients, but friends who need their assistance. We all need to convey genuine care and concern to enhance relationships, even when the initial phase of the relationship may be difficult. For example, think about the following scenario:

One Thursday afternoon, Jessica's mom received a phone call from her math teacher. Over the course of the call, it became apparent that Jessica was failing math and not completing her homework. Despite efforts on behalf of the teacher to provide additional academic help, Jessica had shut down and refused to dig her way out.

Naturally, that evening, Jessica's parents set time aside to get her to open up about the struggles in math class. Jessica tried to assure them she had a handle on the situation and did not need help.

As is common in many parent-child interactions, things escalated due to stressors on behalf of everyone involved. In fact, Jessica's parents even hinted to her that she was lying.

The alleged help session between Jessica and her parents erupted into a shouting match and sadly, Jessica stormed off, leaving her parents aggravated and upset.

In building relationships with students and children, teachers and parents need the constant reminder to separate behaviors from identifiers.

Children make mistakes and will continue to make mistakes. It's part of learning and growing, and, more importantly, it is part of creating who they are. Like a child, our persona is built upon the construction of experiences and our interpretation of them. Therefore, we are an integral part of building character in ourselves and each other.

Denis, also, believes in the power of creating positive experiences with people, especially children (as the topic turned toward education):

> It's funny. We have children, and we think you are going to teach them a lot; however, they end up teaching us more about ourselves than we teach them anything, probably because they are a reflection of us. But I also think with children, in my own and in others, it's the values we instill in them may go into a hiding at certain points (not in a good way or a bad way), but we see these core values that weren't clear (at certain times of their lives), and then they are!
>
> These values are now crystal clear when they hit age twenty or thirty, but you were never sure in their early or teen years whether those values took root or not. And so I think that is one of the challenges for all teachers.

Some of the values that are being taught are simple planting the seed for (their later return); we may see pieces of them, and we may not. We may never be sure, but the work may be amazing! Outstanding! And create a product that we may never know (but it's there).

The key to this ideal, according to Denis, lies within the conversation. To truly know and understand someone, we must first be willing to listen to their story, to talk with them openly and honestly, and to agree or disagree with dignity and respect. In order to accomplish this task, we must first be willing to push aside our bias that can and does stop conversations before they start.

THE FOCUSED HEART: OWN THE START!

As Denis stated so perfectly, "We can only change one behavior in this life, that's our own. We can't change somebody else's behavior; we can only change our own behavior with the hope that our behavior will alter the behavior of others we are trying to teach or move."

It is easy to magnify negative interactions with folks and make issues of incidences or mountains out of molehills, as some would say. Develop a healthier perspective where you continue to have hope for all people. As human beings, we must have the courage to embrace the interactions enough to confront them. Yet, we must also hold loosely to them and let them go if need be.

Call it *clean slating*. Everyone deserve to be clean slated every day and sometimes several times within a day. Compartmentalizing their negative behaviors so the behaviors do not infect the next interaction is monumental in gaining the respect and trust of students. As Denis stated, "What does that person need? And how can I adjust my behavior to get them to the place where they are adjusting their behavior or action?"

NOTE

1. All Denis P. O'Brien quotes presented in this chapter are from an in-person interview with the authors that took place on April 27, 2018.

13

Silence Is Golden—Perfect for the Theater, Not for Life!

Recognize the Power of Response

> Unless we as professionals, understand how to be effective communicators and how to engage our audience to captivate people's hearts and minds, we risk silence being misinterpreted.
>
> —William J. Marrazzo, *president and CEO, WHYY, Inc.*[1]

Did you ever think about the typical dinner table discussion with your family? Nowadays, people are "on the go" so much with sports and other activities, it sometimes becomes difficult to actually have that sit-down experience. But on the rare occasions when our families do dine together, the conversations are frank and always full of interesting themes.

Interestingly, most of our conversations do not focus on the actual task or activity from the day, but more of the conversations surrounding the actions. In simple terms, when we stop and think about the dialogue, the content more often focuses on other conversations rather than the actual pursuit. For example, in our houses, many of our chats revolve around what our children heard from their teachers or from other students. These conversations engage both us and the kids, as they provide a support network for both positive and not so positive experiences with other human beings.

One of the key components to this situation (and others) is our response to our children when they do indeed bring about situations they want to discuss. Candidly, the outward journey of our heart with our children, students, colleagues, or staff is best navigated when we bring a positive, confident persona to the circumstance. Therefore, our ability to constructively and positively respond to actions and comments puts relationships on a positive trajectory. More importantly, the construction of positivity gives our audience their own story to tell by allowing the initial conversation to be authenticated.

Now, the latter may seem like academic blather, but hopefully the following example puts those words into context. Suppose an employee had an issue with a customer and was conversing about it with her manager. Perhaps she was upset, as often times confrontations with customers can be, especially when we are trying to be supportive among a plethora of, say, complaints or sometimes insults. If the manager, after hearing the employee's story, dismisses it quickly with a response like, "That's the job, kid. Better get used to it," chances are she won't feel better about the situation or her involvement with the customer. Once more, the lack of supporting and positive message from the manager certainly does not build an extension of the heart, which, in turn, can cause the employee to become disconnected from both the manager and the company ("I surely won't share the next negative experience if this is the type of help I am going to receive").

Now, if we take that same situation and switch just a few words to the response, the entire trajectory of both the conversation and the extension of the heart gains positive momentum. Instead of dismissing the feelings of the employee, a simple, "I can understand how you are feeling. It can be tough sometimes dealing with people who are upset, but it sounds like you did an excellent job remaining calm."

Needless to state, our ability to affirm one's feelings, especially in times of distress, goes a long way in securing another's confidence and our relationship with each other. Bill Marrazzo, president and CEO of WHYY, Inc., knows the importance of positive response. Having worked in the communications business for many years, Bill realizes that "the right words" are critical to the right message.

Bill sees one of the responsibilities of leaders, teachers, and employees is to cultivate a skill set that affirms relationships. For example, Bill stated that "I have grown to appreciate that, unless and until, you develop soft skills with a colleague, or in your case between a teacher and a student, until those soft skills and expectations are developed, everything on a transactional basis gets sub-optimized." In this fashion, having that set of tools that allows us to build lasting relationships is the glue that holds any successful company together. And these tools can take many forms.

During our discussion, Bill described one of his techniques when dealing with this topic:

> Now here's an example: I have never worked for an enterprise, ever, where I have personally *not* written a handwritten note to every new employee.
>
> Like when the sun rises in the morning, it is what I get up and do. It has been remarkable to me how those very modest gestures have had a gigantic impact on new employees, or as I am about to make the case, a new student in a classroom who somehow begins to see the leadership of the enterprise or the leadership of the classroom, i.e. the teacher, in a very different way.
>
> It's a small technique that has been proven in the communication realm. And at worst, it sets up a situation where the CEO (or in your case, the teacher), the person responsible, for the enterprise is seeing the human quality side of it. I don't know honestly if a teacher has the time in between academic years to drop a note to each of their new

students coming into their classroom, but I am sure there are ten ways to spin that idea, many ways that it could become easier to get it done.

I guess with that sort of example, let me say one more thing. . . . I am perpetually mindful that unless you are communicating honestly and effectively with anyone . . . unless we have a small bucket of techniques we use to develop a relationship with employees or students, on a non-transactional basis, everything else becomes too complicated to get done well.

Therefore, I work hard in between transactions, in between budgets, in between public hearings, in between the inevitable crisis (because they come at you frequently) with individuals at a one on one level, so that when the crisis does hit or when the transaction is due, there's a reservoir of goodwill and understanding between two people, that makes the management of that transaction, as unpleasant as it may be, a bit more productive.

As Bill alluded to, we are bombarded with daily interactions. Of course, it is within our power to discern how we will attend to these interactions. And, of course, there are times when we choose not to attend at all. However, fast-forward that choice. How will the family dinner table discussion go for the child whose attempt to interact with us fell on deaf ears? Perhaps the child will not talk at all, or perhaps the child will share that an attempt was made to have a conversation, but there was only silence. Silence.

Insignificant are the actions of a day when compared to our personal responses to those actions.

Words can create moments; moments can blossom and magnify into a mood, an attitude that we ourselves might not benefit from, but someone else could. There is immense power in responding to people in a manner that is positive and heartfelt. Planting a seed with what we say gives the other person something to talk about later to a friend or family member. In other words, *use your response as a catalyst to continue a conversation beyond your realm of knowing.* When we ignore or respond passively to a person, the motivation for that human being to re-engage a second or third time diminishes.

When we were discussing the essence of this chapter, Bill reflected upon an experience he had with a teacher who had a profound impact on him:

I had a 7th grade social studies teacher, who, every day, every class, would articulate his three personal/professional values: "this is why I am doing this." And it stuck with me—somehow made it possible for me to get thru that class differently and maybe even more effectively because he put himself as a human out on the line and by the way, that is not to say he was not a disciplinarian because he was [laugh]. But he was one of the first teachers I had who expressed himself the way that I understood why he was teaching, why he had chosen teaching.

Bill's narrative holds true for us as well. We have all had that teacher that made the difference for us. The key is that teacher could be the employee at WHYY or the hoagie maker at Wawa, or the ticket lady at the ballpark. The point is, anyone who holds to these values, who has their mind focused on being a positive force in life, can extend their hearts to another, and by communicating this appreciation for all human beings, we can begin to not only "grow the company," but ourselves as human beings.

The challenge lies in having the time and stamina to actively and constructively respond. The best argument for that is to imagine not responding, and the damage that the passive, disengaged response can have on a person. We have to be responsible for creating a pattern of communication that breeds respect and builds relationships. We cannot limit our communication vehicle simply to oral, face-to-face engagements. That is the pressure we create for ourselves.

For example, consider this classroom narrative:

Maria has been chatting with you about a new puppy she picked out over the weekend; as she is telling you all about it, the bell rings, a student interrupts you to hand in homework, and numerous students are yelling goodbye to you and asking last-minute questions such as, do we have homework? Before you know, Maria has left the classroom, is hurrying down the hall to math class, and your next class is coming in.

For a split second, you consider how rude that must have looked to Maria, but new faces are engaging with you and the next class is starting. The day progresses and you forget all about Maria by 3:00.

But, Maria has not forgotten. She saunters into the house after a long bus ride and gloomily sits down on the couch. Her mom immediately questions her dismay and asks her what happened. She is confused why her daughter would be so sad; after all, they selected a puppy and were heading out to pick it up in a few days.

Maria proceeds to explain that no one cares about the puppy. She explains that she tried to tell her teacher about the puppy and she never responded, she ignored her. (Although the teacher felt overwhelmed by the barrage of questions and comments that morning, Maria only heard her own voice. She thought the conversation was just between her and her teacher.) Maria's honest perception is actually a misperception, but it's real to Maria. The lack of words and response from her teacher created a foul mood for Maria and affected her outlook.

Consider vehicles of communication that are efficient in meeting the emotional needs of students, of all people. Using Bill's idea here would have been amazing—Maria would have left school with a heart that *grew three sizes* if you had slipped her a note that simply said *Maria, loved your story about the puppy! Want to hear more about it tomorrow!* It takes milliseconds to write it, but the power of the response is infinite.

Our ability to respond timely to people speaks to our empowerment as leaders. At the end of the day, there is peace and security knowing we recognized the power of response.

THE FOCUSED HEART: OWN THE RESPONSE

Brainstorm and prepare ways you can effectively and efficiently communicate with people so no one leaves feeling unattended or ignored. Consider preparing note cards in advance with a template and design that is quick to fill in and send to a student, each employee, customers, and so on. with phrases such as *I care about . . .* or *I want to hear more about . . .* or *I am sorry I did not hear the rest of. . . .* Keep the notes brief but meaningful. Be mindful that how you respond feeds the relationship.

Bill also had another excellent idea to share regarding this topic. He stated that "I had a music teacher who, to kind of keep everybody on their toes or off guard or anticipating the unanticipated, he would teach music from the back to the front of the music itself. He would go backwards. And his theory was, you can't really explore the pathway in any score until you know how it resolves in the end—you need to know the end of the story. He would teach the music backwards. Now I don't know if his fundamental philosophy was true or not, but it was a very non-traditional way of teaching music, and it certainly redefined my expectation of that teaching experience."

In this regard, perhaps anticipating a future conversation may indeed spark a positive feeling in someone. We know how good it feels when we visit *our* (did it again) *Wawa* and the counter folks already know to check the hazelnut for us. Having a knowledge of others, no matter how small, demonstrates a caring component to our personalities and the relationship we want to create with others.

Within the first seven chapters, the focus was to "know thy self." Now, our focus must be to know others as ourselves. Our responses, even as simple as listening (which is not so simple), do just that.

NOTE

1. All William J. Marrazzo quotes presented in this chapter are from a phone interview with the authors that took place on March 26, 2018.

14

What Floor Is Your Mood Elevator On?

Inspire through Illuminating

> I control what mood I am in. I can either be dissatisfied with something or I can do something about it. The influence that I personally have is directly linked with how people interact with me, react; and how I interact and give positive examples and feedback.
>
> —Thomas Mehler, *president, Southco, Inc.*[1]

Coach Bruce was your straightforward, hockey coach. Father to two boys on the team, Coach B volunteered to spend his weekends (and three nights a week) on the ice, teaching his young players about the basics of playing hockey. Although the competition was intense on the travel circuit, Coach B always made sure the boys understood that the purpose of playing sports was not to win or lose but to improve their skills, make friends, have fun, exercise, and so on. Obviously, the parents on the team, for the most part (there is always one or two that want to win at any cost), appreciated his demeanor and treatment of these young lads.

One of Bruce's famous lines came from his pregame speeches. Again, as a dad with a full-time job and a family, Bruce's hockey skills were average, but his life skills were amazing. Coach would always tell the boys that there are only two things in the entire game that are in our control—our attitude and our effort. Throughout the season, there were many times when the team was down in a game, and parents could hear Coach B yell from the bench, "Attitude and effort, boys! Attitude and effort." Although the boys did not win every game when the battle cry was invoked, they sure did work to give their best effort for themselves, their coach, and each other.

When we think about this short tale, the words "attitude" and "effort" resound, as the focus of this chapter deals with control. Thomas Mehler, President of Southco, was certainly illuminating with his words, and much of his advice echoed the tenets of our hockey example.

There is great power in the human ability to ignite others through words and through presence; it stems from our inner energy that is self-created and self-sustained. In our interactions, we must strive to be the person who brings illuminations to our environments. We can build and maintain relationships with people through the positive influence we bring every day. But make no mistake, there is a choice to be made.

Thomas explains the same ideal in his brief account of common conversations he has with staff members, "When I talk to employees, I tell them there are two things I believe in. The first is a scientific fact, and the other is a belief. First, I do not believe that when people get up in the morning, they are going to tell themselves 'I'm going to go to work today, and I'm going to do a really poor job.' So in general, I believe everyone desires to do a good job. What gets in the way is life (and our reactions to the circumstances surrounding it).

The second idea which I believe is scientific fact—the human brain has infinite capacity to learn. What gets in the way is life or attitude or whether we want to put the effort in and some people need longer and learn differently than others."

In Thomas's comments, we witness the pattern of control and our ability to rise above the negative influences that can shatter our chances to make good, great! Much of this optimistic outlook has to do with our persona and desire to not succumb to negativity.

Extensive research has been done to study the ingredients to a persona that is powerful, attractive, motivating, and seemingly magical. Despite the perceptions of many, the persona is not one of beauty, good looks, intelligence, and perfect physique. According to professor of leadership and organizational psychologist Ronald Riggio, PhD, charisma is comprised of three main ingredients: expressiveness, control, and sensitivity. Riggio adds, "A lot of charisma comes down to how you communicate. It's your ability to pick up on other's people's emotions as well as express your own."[2]

In the classroom or mailroom, we gauge the emotions of people all day long and in split seconds we determine how to respond; we are a master at interacting with people, **but there is a disparity between merely interacting with people and building relationships.** The emotional investment elevates the interaction to a relationship; the stamina to continue doing so day in and day out speaks to your personal emotional endurance.

Riggio defines expressiveness as "a talent for spontaneously striking up conversations and easily conveying feelings." Others might call this the "woo factor."

In education, striking up conversations is not optional; it is something we are immersed in all day long! But think how often we *avoid* striking up a conversation with a student or colleague because we anticipate a negative outcome? Consider the gloomy student or the pouty colleague. You cheerily greet a colleague with a simple "How are you?" The emotionally eroded colleague responds, "Just dandy," expressed with the utmost sarcasm; hidden meaning: "Terrible, I'd rather be anywhere but here."

Despite that response, we make it a point every day to be expressive and convey our best self to that person, as we do with everyone else. **Allowing the attitudes and demeanors of others to determine our actions is not charismatic.** Lock into people with your energy and zest for life; don't reduce yourself to the negative tones and climates around you.

The second ingredient defined by Riggio is control or *the ability to fine-tune your persona to fit the mood and social makeup of any group*. Notice that it does not say *the social makeup and mood of a group define you*. It is easy to allow the mood of a group to negatively permeate into our persona. Having a calm control of who we are despite group mood pressure is critical to charisma. The term *fine-tune* is key in the definition.

We can show empathy by fine-tuning our persona, but completely adjusting who we are and sacrificing our own mood to fit that of the group is not demonstrative of control. Control is derived from our ability to read a situation, and the emotions there within, and tactfully respond or assimilate. Connecting with the audience with a controlled, secure stance brings richness and encouragement to an audience. We may know people with this character trait; they exude a calmness in addition to a fiery energy; it's balanced meticulously.

Thomas calls this the "mood elevator." As in the opening quote, we hold the power of what "floor" we choose to reside on. In simple terms, it is our selection of our destination, along with the manner that we take upon our journey, which defines not only the entire trip, but our person in the process. In Thomas's words, "So how we interact to people is not so much what we say, it's the how that matters more, with that, you get not just peoples body, meaning their arms or their brains, whatever they use to do their work with, you also in their heart. **You can only in their heart when they feel you care about them.** If you don't care about them, that means you don't care. And whether this is the reality or just a perception doesn't really matter; if they feel that you don't care about them, they won't care about you or your business."

With this understanding, Riggio's third element of sensitivity, as defined as *a gift for listening and figuring out other people's mindsets*, is crucial in the process of completing ourselves.

We all have influential power, but the influence is derived from our ability to connect with people, to prioritize our passion and make it contagious to the audience. Appealing to students or staff means that sometimes we pause "the planned conversation" to propose an idea or discuss an issue from our moral compass, taking time out to talk about life quality and its journey. In the educational world, we call this the "teachable moment," and it works in business as well.

A collective group of students unprepared for class prompts us to have an open conversation about responsibility; a story of violence or tragedy in the news prompts others to have a conversation about tolerance and acceptance of differences in an effort to sustain peace. **Our sensitivity to each other elicits a shared vision and inspires those around us to get on board and travel in a courageous direction.**

Lee Iacocca, a charismatic leader for Chrysler in the late 1970s, encouraged his staff by stating, "Motivation is everything. You can do the work of two people, but you can't be two people. Instead, you have to inspire the next guy down the line and get him to inspire his people." On the days we feel least energized to get into the school building and illuminate and inspire, be mindful that each gift of motivation we bring gradually motivates someone else, and in the long run, the outcome is exponential. More people are doing the *work* we initiated; leaders are created and more students and staff are animated.

Thomas had an interesting story along the lines of taking that positive first step in initiating a meaningful relationship, even if it was going to be temporary:

> I had an example of a colleague who told me the worst thing for him is he goes on an airplane and he sits and somebody in front of him puts the airplane seat back. And he hates it, and he pushes back, right? And, I can relate to him, I am very tall. So, one day one guy stood up after he pushed back and he realized that the person is really, really tall and then there was another gentleman who sat there and he said to him, I will make a deal with you, if you don't put your seat back, I will pay for all of your drinks on the flight. The other person replied, you know you don't have to do that, but I appreciate it and I won't put my seat back. Again, the way the guy interacted with him caused a positive reaction. You see? And I think that's the key to employee engagement, its positive management but you have clear accountabilities and clear behavioral guidelines, we call it our cultural beliefs.

THE FOCUSED HEART: OWN YOUR ATTITUDE

Evaluate your persona for charisma. In what facets of the day do you struggle to be expressive, in control and sensitive? Look for personalities around you who exemplify charisma and begin to adopt traits to illuminate others.

Have an honest conversation with yourself about the changes you need to make to be more inspirational. Remove the misperceptions that inspirational people are those who look like Brad Pitt, George Clooney, Julia Roberts, or Heidi Klum, and focus on true inner traits of leaders. You don't have to be in charge of a committee or a company to acquire leadership traits. Remember that leaders establish a following and develop new leaders; educators with an authentic, positive influence over students are leaders.

Let the words of Sir Winston Churchill be a beacon and resonate, "We are all worms, but I believe I am a glowworm."

Additionally, realize that *your* persona matters. For example, consider Thomas's tale concerning rank and influence in companies and schools:

> If I tell you the janitor has as much influence on the success of the company as the CEO, you probably can't relate to it but if you really think about it, if the janitor stops cleaning the bathrooms, after a week or two, the employees will really get upset about it but they're not going to blame the janitor, they are going to blame the company. 95 percent of people would never say anything; they would just become more irritated, disgruntled, disengaged, and therefore not caring. Things would get out that are bad

and therefore have a negative influence on the company. It's the same with us right, if we go to a restaurant and we have a bad meal, we don't blame the chef, we blame the restaurant. If we have bad service, we don't blame the waiter, we just don't go back, and most of us just don't go back.

And it might be only that the waiter or the chef had a bad day. And so it's making people understand, no matter where they are on the ladder that they do have an impact on this company and that we do want their hearts and we do want them to care because we care about them as well. They need to see that connection and that they actually have an impact. They are needed; everybody wants to have a meaning in life. No matter what we do. And to see that meaning, and to see that connection to the bigger picture, you get their heart because everybody wants it.

Likewise, do not be afraid to explore options to promote a positive workplace experience. Thomas reminds us, "In the old world, it was more looking for safety, order and promotion for self, now a lot of them look for hey, what can I learn, is it challenging, can I learn something new? Do I enjoy it? Do I have a purpose? Does the company have a purpose? Can I connect what I do to a purpose? Am I in a caring environment?" Bringing a "can do" attitude can enhance our ability to stay curious, even when we fail. The process is critical for those who wish to maintain a spirit of high energy and a positive demeanor.

Remember Coach Bruce—attitude and effort. That's what we can and do control.

NOTES

1. All Thomas Mehler quotes presented in this chapter are from a phone interview with the authors that took place on June 15, 2018.

2. Ronald Riggio, as quoted in Jessica Winter's "How to Light Up a Room," *O, The Oprah Magazine*, October 2012 Issue; also available on Oprah.com: http://www.oprah.com/spirit/the-science-behind-charisma-and-confidence/all.

Part III
AN IMPACTFUL JOURNEY OF THE HANDS

Beyond the corporate and classroom walls, we want to leave a positive, igniting legacy. With the end in mind, we teach, work, and relate to others with intention: our leadership serves both academic and inspirational purposes. Knowing that our legacy is a gift to others: igniting people, igniting change, and igniting a greater purpose. With a focused self and heart, outreach of the hands becomes a natural extension of who we are, impacting the greater community.

15

Just Napkins? Come On, You Can Do Better Than That!

Support and Serve

> Time is money so time spent in service to others is currency of the heart.
> —Nicholas J. Giuffre, *former president and CEO, Bradford White Corporation*[1]

"Charity begins at home and every parent and all teachers should guide children towards the pleasure of helping others. I am living by the philosophy that the first third of your life you learn, the second third of your life you earn, and the last third of your life you give back. Although you probably are in a much better position to give back financially during the last third of your life, the first and second thirds could be so much more fulfilling if you start small and then grow in your philanthropy. Giving back is never limited to a financial donation. Your life will be so satisfying if the gift of giving starts early and continues throughout your entire life."

So I guess we could end this chapter right now, as Bradford White Corporation's former CEO Nick Giuffres's initial statement on the topic of service captures every ounce of what we felt when we thought about this chapter. Of course, the publishers would not be too thrilled about stopping right here. But the point serves well—giving is the backbone to a centered life, and those who realize this at an early age carry the secret of life with them wherever it takes them.

It is funny how when we are asked to complete a resume, we truly begin to inventory our service impact. Please do not feel bad at this point, as our resumes could use additions as well. Interestingly, as educators, we encourage our students to serve in the school and be involved in extracurricular activities, but our own picture can often be devoid of supportive and serving roles. Committees to which we have been assigned (despite our better intentions) or additional roles with supplemental pay are outside of the realm of true serving. Therefore, being told we *have* to lead the safety committee does not count as *voluntary* serving.

Supporting and serving others can be described as putting our hearts in motion. Some may say that those in the service industry support and serve every day. As mentioned previously in the text, we are in the industry of generous giving—that is true! But conversations with folks about serving really puts the fire right in our face.

Did you ever engage in a conversation with a student who exuberantly tells you about his weekend activity of building homes for Habitat for Humanity? Or describes how he went on a retreat for his church where he served meals to the homeless? Or portrays the garden that she planted at the local children's park? We listen to these stories with awe, and we praise the students' efforts and their love for others. Then the burning question surfaces: **Have you ever done anything like that?**

For a moment, we run a fast rewind of our life, trying to recall the last time we served others—not for money or because it was required—but because we wanted to make a difference. We think to ourselves, "I can't tell her I don't have time, I can't say I teach and that is enough service, and I can't just say no. What impression would I leave on her if I just said no?"

The reality is that we are making impressions upon students every day by who we are, what we do, and how we elect to use our free time. Impressionable students seek out lifestyles that are admirable, and teachers play a large role in student lives, so we are bound to be role models. But are we not all role models for the brief time that a customer or employee is in our presence? Are we not, at that moment, the only human being in the world that matters to that individual?

In the words of Martin Luther King Jr., "Everybody can be great, because anybody can serve."[2] We know the greatest excuse: time. However, we can make the time to serve in some capacity, even through the slightest of gestures.

Nick, believes that charity starts from the top:

> Corporate giving starts right at the top! If you are the CEO, you will set the example of corporate and personal charity. There are so many wonderful charities that deserve support, it would be impossible to serve them all. As CEO, I have, with input from our employees, chosen to support major charities like the Boys & Girls Club, LLS, Susan Komen, by either donating financially or volunteering time at their fundraising events. Our company tries to generate as much brand awareness in the community with charity as we do in advertising dollars. It sends a message not only to the employees, but to all potential customers that our company is a caring and a giving back corporation in our community.

These examples are tremendous ways that an entire company can get behind an initiative to support a greater cause in the community. Nick had also mentioned that sometimes efforts start small, but turn into huge initiatives. For example, his chairman recently "asked everyone to start saving tabs from cans so we could donate them to the local Ronald McDonald House. And just by him making that small request, we have been able to fill up many huge containers to donate, and the Ronald McDonald is always overwhelmed at how many tabs we are able to collect. We have had so much fun and satisfaction filling up these containers, it was an easy and fun way to send the message to our employees of how important it is to give back in any way possible."

Another example of giving small can occur through our children and their activities. For instance, both of us have children that play on multiple sports teams. And let us tell you, the *Sign-Up Genius* website is one that frequents our inbox numerous times in the course of a week. Truthfully, there are many times we think to ourselves, "I don't have time to do one more thing!" Nonetheless, not to be outed as "that family," we ultimately make our selection of napkins or pretzel logs and move on with the day's events.

However, in putting our hands in motion, perhaps we should consider elevating our efforts next time. In other words, what is the real reason we never select homemade cookies? We don't have the time? We can't cook? Napkins are easier and mindless? Somebody has to do napkins, it might as well be me? Perhaps all of those justifications fit; we really want to be the permanent napkin person! Yet, think of the smiles when you take off that big napkin to reveal those delicious cookies! Now, that's an unexpected treat worth the time.

Again, this is a tremendous way to put our passion into action when it comes to assisting our teammates (Yes! Just as kids are teammates, the parents of those kids are teammates, too, and we need to act as such.) Yet, as both Nick mentioned and we concurred, actions of the heart are just as important when it comes to extending our hands. In other words, sometimes the greatest gift we can give a person is companionship or a listening ear.

Generosity is not limited to outward actions; our ears can be our hands.

There is an elder man that hangs out at *My Wawa* (we will let you guess if it is Joy's or Tony's). Often times, I rush by, as sometimes my internal clock does not align with the actual one. Needless to say, school is not going to wait for me. One day, though, I did have an extra moment and took a chance of saying "hi" to this elderly man. Turns out, his name is Joe, and he was one of the original graduates of our school. The conversation, though brief, was pretty amazing, and I went to work thinking about him the entire day.

The very next day, I made sure I got up a couple minutes early to be able to chat with him. I did and have been for the last eight and a half years! As I learned, Joe is a great person, and he just loves to talk to people. He says that he "sees the world" at Wawa, and he chooses to hang out there. Sadly, my assumption of Joe prior to knowing him was that he was either not well or economically unstable. Neither was true. It was not until I adjusted my mind and opened my heart that I was able to extend my hands (or in this case) my ears to a fellow human being who was just looking for connection.

Starting a legacy of service that not only serves the task but supports your personal stretch to give is a choice. The concept of support and serve as a legacy does not mean doing what you have always done. Just as we push ourselves to perform better or stronger in a workout, we must push ourselves to serve differently and in a greater capacity. As simple as this might sound, we should consider the domino effect that it will have.

If you begin to elevate your giving from napkins to homemade cookies, someone else who struggles to serve can begin to donate napkins. This simplistic, mundane example reflects the concept of upgrading giving to open up more opportunities for giving from others. In this fashion, we are moving away from the safe, comfortable zone where we have always been and stretching ourselves to do more, but our gift then becomes twofold.

We are giving to a cause on a grander scale, and we are encouraging other donors. Our election not to choose the secure zone enables someone else to begin giving. Our support of the volunteer structure evokes more volunteers—a win-win! Here, there is greater leverage that arises from a giving heart; it identifies how we choose to live the example we believe.

In our society, technology has overtaken our time, especially in our students. Look around. Everyone is on their phones. Parents and students both would agree that the digital, virtual world monopolizes a large portion of student time and students are not only disinterested in service projects, but they claim they don't have time. Recent research has revealed that teens spend close to nine hours a day in front of a screen and more than two-thirds of teenagers own a personal phone. Face-to-face interactions have been replaced with screens. Parents are not surprised by this research, and teachers are probably thinking the numbers might even be higher.

In the classroom, we understand that social media is the thread that weaves student interactions together and sometimes as a disservice to the emotional well-being of students. We directly or indirectly hear stories of who said what to whom and the tension that correlates with the drama. Students appear to have an enormous amount of time committed to social media, yet students will be the first to tell us they don't have time for an assignment or time for test preparation.

Whenever you get the opportunity, have a conversation with your children about the amount of time they devote to serving others instead of themselves. Tell them that *to be about life, don't make life all about them*. Most students don't even realize they are making life all about them; they just go through day to day, moment by moment with a focus on their own personal priorities. The best way to get them to steer away from screen time might be to get them to look outside of themselves and start living life for others.

Gandhi, with great clarity, stated, "The best way to find yourself is to lose yourself in the service of others." Turning kids away from the drama of social media is only half the game; the other half is to turn them on to service and support of those around them. To boost their love and appreciation for people requires face-to-face interactions with people who will admire them for who they are and what they offer.

THE FOCUSED HANDS: OWN YOUR EFFORTS

As we are in the educational field, Nick boasted much about the impact that his teachers had on him. He stated that "A teacher who volunteers to coach a team or supervise a club, who teaches music and theatre during and after school programs and stays late to help tutor a child who is struggling with school or other home life is one who makes a difference. They are the change makers who will help shape a student's life far after the bell rings to end class!"

Again, we hope these efforts are completed with the genuine spirit of assisting our children and not just for the paycheck. Truth be told, the checks for extracurricular activities never ever match the number of hours we place into the activity. Therefore, let's just say that those who go above and beyond, that allow students to see a different side of themselves outside the classroom, are the change makers in schools. But being a change maker is not limited to education.

Despite how we feel in a day, know that the perception of many is that "being nice" is our job. They admire what we do, but they also know that we are being paid for what we do. By being a person who serves and supports in other ways, we can truly demonstrate to our customers that we recognize the power of volunteering, of extending our hands for others. We can genuinely be a living example of *being about life*.

By setting a few escalated goals to upgrade our service to others, we will discover that it is not only easy to do, but very rewarding and fulfilling. Whatever we have done in the past, do a little bit more—choose to bring the home-baked cookies, not the napkins.

NOTES

1. All Nicholas J. Giuffre quotes presented in this chapter are from a written contribution provided to the authors on June 22, 2018.
2. Martin Luther King Jr., "Martin Luther King Jr. Quotes," azquotes.com (quote #343537).

16

But I Really Thought People Liked Hearing Me Complain!

Reflect and Accept

> The Human Spirit is stronger than anything that can happen to it! . . . Why do we wait to implement this valuable gift, when we can utilize it on every obstacle, problem, or challenge that we meet every week or every month?
>
> —Kevin Reilly, *former NFL player, motivational speaker, and author*[1]

Circumstances and people, despite our best attitudes and efforts, do not always leave us with a sense of pride and admiration. As educators, our students both amaze and frustrate us within a day, and we must retain unconditional acceptance to rise above it. Our efforts to converse and communicate with students to develop heartfelt connections aid in our capacity to release the negative tensions and separate the actions from the person.

In life, we must develop an emotional maturity to cognitively choose, yes *choose*, what deserves our energy and what does not. Working with students is a challenging job. Additionally, working with anyone can be difficult if we allow it to be. The personalities we face on Monday are not the same personalities we face on Tuesday. People change, they grow, and they don't have the mature discernment to bring their best every day. Therein lies the challenge of working with human beings.

Kevin Reilly, former NFL player and now motivational speaker, has an incredible, personal story of resilience. In short, Kevin was diagnosed with a desmoid tumor and had to have his left shoulder, arm, and four ribs amputated. He speaks of this and other life occurrences in his recently published book *Tackling Life*.[2]

Obviously, the reality that Kevin faced was not easy, and rest assured doubt, fear, and frustration had many chances to engulf his thinking, leading him to a place of darkness and despair. However, if you know Kevin, you realize that these negative attributes never stood a chance (much like his opponents on the gridiron).

Kevin, although experiencing moments of doubt, consistently surrounded himself with positive people who assisted him with accepting his situation. In this sense, Kevin realized that just because he was an amputee, it would not define him as a person or limit the impact he could have on the world around him.

In his book, Kevin retells a time when Rocky Bleier gave him a call. Many of us know the story of Rocky, drafted by the Pittsburgh Steelers for a short term that was interrupted by a draft into the US Army. Rocky returned wounded from his patriotic mission and faced medical, physical, and emotional challenges but decided not to give in to the face of failure. He fought his way back with determination and drive, becoming one of the Steelers' leading running backs and tasting Super Bowl victories four times! After Kevin's eleven-hour surgery, Bleier reached out to him and gave Kevin some tremendous advice—advice we think encapsulates the essence of this chapter. Rocky said, "Do not let people set the bar of what you can and can't do. That is your job and only your job. You must promise me that you won't quit on anything unless you try it 3 times!"

As we have stated prior, sometimes the giving of ourselves is more important than any monetary value we can muster. The significance of Rocky's advice is enormous for us when it comes to extending our hands. Rocky was able to inspire Kevin to not give in to the attraction of self-pity. So many times, we allow ourselves to reside in the negative for fear of failure. Hence, we not only stop our potential successes by not even trying, we confine our would-be positive influence on someone else and substitute them with a less desirable conversation.

For example, when we encounter a challenging person or situation, an easy choice is to harbor the stress and aggravation and share it out with as many people as possible, garnering support and alliances. Yet consider the energy that we are using for those futile purposes. It's crazy!

Now, imagine our day starting with a circle of energy that we distribute throughout the day. With teaching, unexpected events arise that we don't plan on, but we *know* this, so account for it. If the energy pictorially is contained in a pie chart, slice out your *Be Selfish to Be Generous* piece first, then commit yourself to use all other positive energy for the good of others. In other words, we need to be more cognizant of looking at people, events, and tasks in a day as purposeful, serving, and invigorating. There is little glory in ending a day exhausted from spending negative energy.

Kevin speaks a ton about the power of the human spirit. In us all resides a light that wants to shine through, even in the darkest of times. We have all faced loss or a tragedy of some sort, but as the classic Annie song goes, "The sun will come out tomorrow." Although a bit cheesy (?), please focus upon the context of the message. If we truly believe that the sun will rise again, then the human spirit can never ever be fully confined to utter darkness.

In Kevin's words, "The Human Spirit is stronger than anything that can happen to it!" God gifted every one of us with this unique power, but we mostly leave it undiscovered until we are faced with a life or death illness or catastrophic event or challenge. Why do we wait to implement this valuable gift, when we can utilize it on every obstacle, problem, or challenge that we meet every week or every month? We don't have to wait! Here is my consent process for channeling resilience since 1979. It is an affirmation list with a few famous quotes and some of my own experiences that I keep in my daily planner to remind me about this God given gift:

Affirmation List
- Don't panic → A calm head wins every time. This too shall pass.
- Control your anger → You lose every time that you get angry!
- Don't hate or hold grudges → Don't let hate or revenge rent the limited space in your head because they then squeeze out happiness and peace. You cannot house both.
- Don't argue with opinionated people → Life is too short to deal with these people. There is an old saying, "Never wrestle with a pig, you will get dirty, and the pig will like it." Keep this renter out of your brain.
- Set goals → "If you aim at nothing you will hit it every time." Reach beyond your expectations!
- Have a plan to reach those goals → Make a reasonable plan (like a GPS map) to guide you to your goals. If it's worth doing and it's important, it's got to be done right now.
- Persistence → Patience is a virtue but persistence to your goals is a blessing.
- Down time and meditation → (Brain breaks.) A fifteen-minute midmorning and a fifteen-minute midafternoon break, without any noise or stimulation, will do wonders for your mind and get you back on track.
- Prayer → There is an old saying that "More things have been wrought by prayer than any person could ever imagine." Control what you can control and let God handle the rest. I believe in this completely! "God will help you move mountains, just make sure you bring your own wheelbarrow."

This list provides a great start to ensuring that our hands are connected to our heart and mind.

As stated prior, an easy way we escape from conflict resolution is to hold a grudge or to harbor ill feelings against others, especially with people who are challenging us day after day. Giving energy to grudges and frustrations robs us of the energy we need for the more passionate slices in our day. Ironically, we expel emotional energy when we retain a grudge toward a person or circumstance. In effect the damage is only affecting us, not the other person.

We can be an emotional prisoner inside our own body when we choose to navigate energy toward negative people. It is within our ability to release the grudge, making us stronger, setting us free, free to give more to others.

In the past, we may have made the mistake of harboring a relationship gone awry and permitting it to affect our daily moods and interactions with others. Gradually, we began to realize that we are in complete control of where we put our energy every day—both physically and emotionally. When people ask us whether or not the situation upsets us, we want to be able to respond with, "Sure, but I don't give it energy anymore."

Many teachers and employees arrive home from school exhausted, complaining about the troubles they had, the stress they endured, and struggling with the inability to release and move on. Everyone and everything suffer because of their negative energy. Reflecting and accepting is a true act of respect for ourselves and for those we serve.

Setting boundaries for ourselves that enables us to accept circumstances for the way they transpired and disciplining ourselves to only give energy to that which is deserving of our energy are crucial to our stamina and outlook. Really consider priorities when we put so much energy into the work day that we have little energy left for our family, home life, pets, and so on.

THE FOCUSED HANDS: OWN YOUR ACCEPTANCE

A critical point in the day to reflect and accept is when we get into our car to leave work and head to the next locale (many times, that is not home). It does not take more than a minute to reflect on the day and accept that we did our best and we are not going to punish ourselves, anyone, or anything beyond that moment. We must prioritize our overall emotional health because everyone deserves the best you; if you are feeling hindered and deflated, you will be less for others and will not be able to see their greatness. Departing from the workplace lot is a pivotal moment to compartmentalize and make you a better you.

As Kevin alliterates, "When a crisis occurs in your life or maybe just a temporary obstacle, how quickly and fully it takes a person to recover from that event or episode is called resilience. Having this quality of being resilient, as a person, can have many positive outcomes for leading a happy and fulfilled life." Grasping that resilience, as flowing as the air we breathe, is one of the keys to moving on from a situation that might otherwise hold us in the negative. Reinvent yourself when change is asking us to do so. It's a choice, and you own it.

NOTES

1. All Kevin Reilly quotes presented in this chapter are from a written contribution provided to the authors on May 23, 2018.

2. Kevin Reilly, *Tackling Life: How Faith, Family, Friends, and Fortitude Kept an NFL Linebacker in the Game* (Downingtown, PA: Faith & Family Publications, 2017).

17

Passing the Mashed Potatoes and Saying "Thank You," It Really Is That Simple!

Appreciate and Encourage

> Every time you extend your hand, you touch somebody's heart.
>
> —Phil Martelli, *former head men's basketball coach,*
> *St. Joseph's University*[1]

Some of the greatest coaches of all time used their words to motivate their teams to accomplish unbelievable goals. This is not to say that being a tactician is not valuable, if one does not have the Xs and Os down, the chance of being successful wanes. However, being able to communicate the goals of the team through the spoken word is often thought of as a gift. Yet, there are those who would say that this gift is a trait that can be learned by doing the work required to first building an active ear.

In a sense, a collaborative team on a field is a direct match to a collaborative team in a building, and words we use with our students, colleagues, and customers really do matter.

Like coaches, we appreciate and encourage our players with the hope that they will continue the cycle of appreciation through their words and actions.

One of the finest speakers we have come in contact with is Phil Martelli, the Former Head Men's Basketball Coach at St. Joseph's University. Phil is not only an amazing coach, but a person that "walks the walk" when it comes to genuine care and compassion for his fellow human being. Phil's words to us echoed the mantra of not only this section (Extending Our Hands), but the entire text.

Phil believes that "We excite people, we encourage people, by first and foremost, building real relationships." In being a college basketball coach, one of Phil's job responsibilities is to recruit players to the university. In other words, Phil has to compete with literally hundreds of other universities to try to "sell" a player to leave their family and play for his team. Certainly, this is no easy task, when there are so many quality institutions in the world.

Phil, of course, believes that St. Joseph's is an incredible university and what the school has to offer a scholar athlete speaks for itself. But what we have learned is that the process of recruitment can have just as much to do with the "stuff" as it has to do with people at the university.

Feel and fit are topics we speak about with our students when we chat about choosing a college. Assumedly, these are the same types of conversations that coaches have on recruitment trips to high-powered athletes. When we considered the idea of feel and fit, we could not help but to connect it with relationships and Phil's words:

> You want to excite somebody? Extend your hand. Think about all the times in your life, you extend your hand. We shake, we hug, when somebody's down and out, you reach in your pocket and then extend your hand, maybe even before your time, families used to sit and have dinner every night and what did they do? They extended their hand because they passed the potatoes and they passed the bread and they passed the rolls, they passed the meat. They passed it. Every time you extend your hand, you touch somebody's heart.

These words are truly powerful, and they connect to the essence of the moment when Phil (or any of us) meets someone for the first time. Building appreciation and encouragement starts by building trust. That trust extends from the human connections of genuinely caring for someone, and nothing says "I care about you" more than when we extend our hand to someone.

Phil told an interesting story of a time when he was young and had to learn the lesson of getting to know someone prior to being able to encourage them to action:

> I was a high school coach and I was young, twenty-four years old, I was a head high school coach. And I called to a kid, and he ignored my instruction, so I took him out of the game and I let him have it, just like a teacher would let a student have it for not paying attention, or a businessman or woman would walk away from a vendor or a client because, "this isn't going to work."
>
> I found out after the fact, through this young guy's mother, he was deaf in his left ear, he never heard me. Now was that kid at my house? Yes. Did that kid do part-time work for me? Yes. Was that kid at practice every day? Yes. If you had asked me prior to the phone call from his mother, do I know him? I would say, yes. And in that case, I failed. Because I didn't have a real relationship, because I didn't know what I needed to know about those that you think you know.
>
> And I think it goes for every teacher, every business owner, it goes for every coach. You really have to strive and know, in their world, kid to kid, what's a real relationship? What is a real relationship? You cannot get somebody excited about a task unless you have a real relationship.

In the educational realm, think about our attitude in the school day, not just with students, but with other teachers, the custodial staff, the cafeteria staff, the administration, and so on. If those folks are our team, does our coaching style reflect really "knowing" them? Is it an all-inclusive style, where we see the potential in every player? Do we motivate them and bring out their best? Or do we have an, "It's not my job perspective on leadership and inspiration? It's not my job to worry about the cafeteria staff. Who cares if the assistant principal is happy? It's not my job to worry about the teacher three doors down, I have my own problems."

Closed minds, hearts, and hands create a workplace that is fractured, unwelcoming, and, frankly, not a nice place to be. We know there are people in our buildings who make it evident to everyone that they don't want to be there. Yet, did you ever consider the selfishness of those people? Is their problem, struggle, or negative nature really so important to them that they feel the authority to convey it and bring others down around them? It can be burdensome if we allow it, it can be eroding and unfair. Don't allow that type of outlook to become toxic. We must challenge ourselves to stand strong against the personalities around us that are not uplifting. The more we appreciate and encourage others, the more they more they might actually live up to the climate that we are trying to create.

Living a life with a charismatic and magnetic personality promotes happiness; others are drawn to our presence and want to engage with us. A couple of years ago, an article was published on the seven traits that happy people possess.[2] It is fitting for the classroom because it states that happiness is more about our *perspective* and how we react to things around us. **We must adapt a perspective where in the actions and words of others do not define our happiness.**

Choose to be happy; there is amazing self-control, pride, and ownership in choosing happiness. Many who are not choosing it are more focused on the reasons they are unhappy and where the blame lies. Remember chapter 2? We don't have time to be unhappy; our life span is microscopically short.

Gratitude and an appreciation for the simplicities of life are traits that happy people possess. They don't wish for a more luxurious car; they are happy they have a car at all; they live their own life, not one that is in comparison to others. In speaking with Phil, this was one of his most important points he wanted to share with us when it related to teachers and leaders:

> I think that for exciting people, that person has to know that they have a value to you. So whether it's the kid who's struggling along and you as a teacher can assign them the simplest of tasks, they feel like they have a value because you've trusted them.
>
> In my situation, enthusiasm, mentioning somebody by name, using somebody's name is an invaluable tool in terms of exciting them about a task at hand. I think it's really important for all people to understand, we're on teams our whole lives. That classroom's really a team and it has to work in a fluid kind of way, your school, your faculty—it's a team.
>
> Everybody's a team, in your church, in your charitable endeavors, in your community activities, you're always on teams. In your family, you're always on a team. So on a team, everybody has a responsibility, now the beauty for me, in my opinion, is that those responsibilities can flip. Because, every day that you teach is a good day, but if you also learn that day, it's a great day.

It's a good day when you can teach because you have knowledge, you have emotion, you have character to build, but also I think that everybody from the business leader, the leader at the bank, the pastor at church, whoever it may be, we all have to be open to learning. Because every day that you teach, and every day that you learn is a great day, and they are always available.

As you can tell from this chapter, Phil is a wonderful storyteller, and we would be remiss not to include just one more story/anecdote that again summarizes our influence of people when we get to know them, build trust, challenge them, and teach them. For when these things occur, we find that ultimately, we learn just as much in the process:

I remember a 15-year-old kid; he was a sophomore in high school and I cut him from the team. I was a high school coach at the time, and he wanted to come back and hang around and be a team manager. And, as a junior in high school, he made the JV team and as a senior in high school he made All League. And he went from All League to getting a scholarship in college.

And when people say, well who's the best teacher of basketball? I don't really consider it basketball because that's the game, I'm really coaching and teaching people who love the game. And this young guy taught me. He taught me about don't give up on your dreams, he taught me about having a plan, he taught me about observation because when I asked why he came back, he said the guys you kept had something that I didn't have. So isn't that true in every classroom?

There's gifts in that classroom. Some kid has a gift for dance, and some kid has a gift for math and some kid has a gift for science and they're always being watched. All the kids in that class are watching. The number one salesman at any paper company is being watched by everybody else. And hopefully, in some ways, being emulated. That's really teaching. They're really teaching and they got to their point by learning along the way. So I think every day that you teach and every that you learn—that brings energy. That brings excitement.

In our classroom or job, we have the ability to teach and to learn by first appreciating the relationship we are building with people and by extending our hand in gratitude or service to them. Sometimes that may be a challenge because we don't initially see the potential as Phil described, but as long as the compassion is there, and the genuine spirit to want someone to succeed is there, then we allow the path to stay open for the next attempt at teaching and learning.

THE FOCUSED HANDS: OWN YOUR APPRECIATION

Our gift to appreciate and encourage people around us begins with our ability to coach people with our winning attitude. A winning attitude begins with an emotionally healthy core. Evaluate our emotional health by looking at our level of happiness. What causes happiness to elude us? Making one positive change with ourselves can outwardly alter others. Recognize that coaching others is our gift to our school and community. It has boundless limits.

One of Phil's final comments summarizes this chapter beautifully. Phil stated that "I believe the most powerful statement in the English language is 'Thank You.' And that is an energy boost for people. All the people that we go through the day with, the janitor at school, the cafeteria lady, the bus driver, the little league coach, the dance teacher, the executive secretary, the security guard. You want to see them energized? Right in front of your eye? Look them dead in the eye and thank them. Thank them."

NOTES

1. All Phil Martelli quotes presented in this chapter are from an in-person interview with the authors that took place on May 22, 2018.

2. From an article by Jason DeMers, "7 Traits Only Happy People Have," Inc.com, February 26, 2015: https://www.inc.com/jayson-demers/7-traits-only-happy-people-have.html.

18

Large Coffee, Extra Passion, and Two Heaping Spoonfuls of Creativity!

Experience and Navigate

> Our organizational code is very upside down; it's what we call "serving leadership." We lead by serving. And I think that is what has allowed us to ultimately be really creative because the only mistake you can really make here is not taking the initiative.
>
> —Nick Bayer, *CEO and founder, Saxbys*[1]

People who have the confidence to take risks to strengthen another's life experience will sustain a collective efficacy in life. When we think about this ideal, Nick Bayer is a person that models this type of thinking. As the founder and CEO of Saxbys, Nick is a person who took a risk; however, one would be surprised that his efforts with his company are actually secondary to his core values which guide it.

Nick truly believes in core values (not rules) driving his company. He loves the culture at Saxbys because it is designed to bring out the creativity in people; Nick wants people to TRY and make mistakes. He does not want people to work for him who want to follow a scripted day. As Nick stated, "It's not about whether they can steam milk, can pour espresso shots, we can teach that to anybody. If I can learn that, anybody can learn that. It's about core values, we expect our core values to be everyone's (personal and professional) because then you get to bring your whole self to work every single day."

Would it not be wonderful to work in a place that not only accepts failure, but seeks it out? In our professions, we all look to acquire new skills. In teaching, we are constantly trying to build in different approaches to our instructional practice in order to assist our students in their achievement. We do this also to assist ourselves in maintaining the motivation for the daily grind (pun intended).

As we pondered this premise, we immediately thought of one of Nick's tags that really stuck with us. Nick mentioned that "The mistake of saying, it would be cool if we tried this, and then NOT trying it is the only mistake that's not tolerated here.

We tolerate the mistakes where we say, it would be awesome if we do this, so I am going to plan, set my goal, execute, and I'm going to have the humility to evaluate what went wrong, that's how organizations can harness creativity, harness entrepreneurship but can ultimately be, not just good at what you do, but love what it is that you are doing.

I think that the fact that we are so entrepreneurial, not just by nature, but by design, throughout the organization allows us to naturally be creative. If I run around without that culture, and I started just telling people, 'I want you guys to be creative,' if you have to tell people to be creative, they are not going to be creative. Whereas, if they can just work every single day and not feel like they are boxed in, in any form or format, and they hear the oldest person in the company, me, constantly saying innovate, be entrepreneurial, take risks, make mistakes. If I was twenty-two all over again and in their stage in their career, I think that would be a pretty awesome way to bring my best whole self to work and my creativity, and try to create something."

So do we! But in education or life, it is easy to say that we do not have the liberty to vary our approach because the boss, climate, culture, format, and so on are too strict, too set. Or another convenient excuse we sometimes utilize is the old adage "I don't have time." This one is a personal favorite of ours, because in schools, time is always a bone of contention with folks.

Again, please do not think that we are not just as guilty as the next person when it comes to complaining about time. We are, but the key is recognizing when these excuses are mounting and becoming infectious. Doing our best to stop them before they impact more than our mood elevates our passion and creativity.

In these times, we must take a step back and ask ourselves, "Why are we here?" In other words, what is my mission? We have a friend who is, for lack of a better term, very blunt. In speaking with teachers, he once stated that "if this (teaching) is your second choice for a profession, please do us all a favor and go do your first."

A little on the brash side, but the point is well served. Those who "go through the motions" of their jobs waste their (and ultimately) others' time. For example, we would hope that teachers entered the profession to impart knowledge to students, to care for them, and to make a difference. If, however, the reason for teaching was June, July, and August, then as our friend said, please feel free to extend that summer vacation to a permanent one.

People are smart, and they realize when someone is "mailing it in" on the effort side.

In keeping a proactive, positive approach to our mission, we must ask ourselves, "Do I ignite the minds and hearts of others?" If the honest answer is no, then small (or, in some cases, large) changes might be in order to make our role more invigorating and the students/customers more eager to engage in our persona. And this is how we build and sustain the culture of the hands—by building our own capacity to align with the greater good.

When we asked Nick about this very idea of what is the single greatest component to his company (in terms of its success), he was very quick with his response:

> I would say it's the culture; it's definitely the culture. The fact that we are in the coffee industry is a very sub point to the greater picture here. We are on a mission to make life better; we are on a mission to leverage all the cafés we have, all the jobs we have, all the money we donate, all the corporate partnerships we have, to make the world a better place.
>
> And all of these people, all 555 people, have self-selected to do this business. This isn't me going out there and saying, "John, let me talk you into coming to work for Saxbys." Our people self-select. When they come to an interview, we don't even look at the coffee bar. I could care less if they can tell the difference between a sink and an espresso machine. We can teach them that. But I can't teach someone, to serve yourself by serving others. If someone says, "Nick, that's cool, but I believe the only way you get ahead in life is the dog eat dog world, where you just do what it takes to get ahead," that's great for them. But I don't agree with that, and this isn't the right place for them to work. People self-selected to be a part of this culture.

What an interesting concept this would be for schools. **In other words, what if the students could select you as a teacher?** What do you think your class size would be like? What a reality check; possibly a frightening question to answer! There are some places where schools are trying to build a market mentality. This goes back to the theory that being self-directed affords the learner a greater motivation for success. In simple terms, it means building a system where challenges are constructed by choice instead of by force. This is a pretty bold concept, but one that is becoming an interesting paradigm shift in the way we approach our classrooms. What if we were all special teachers, and the students got to pick us instead of being scheduled into our classrooms? What if those numbers dictated our employment like in business?

Some of the naysayers to this concept believe that some teachers would just give the kids anything they wanted (an "easy A") in order to build numbers. We disagree, however, as we believe with the right leadership and pride, folks would create courses that students not only needed, but wanted because they were dynamic, interactive, useful, and fun.

In education and business, we must change our thinking. One simple adjustment is to raise our level of awareness from the student's/guest's perspective. What is it like to be a student in your class? A guest at your counter? Do you think folks look forward to this experience? Take a curious look at others in your place of employment to see the varied approaches that are keeping people coming back for more. Peer observations for the purpose of acquiring new ideas and strategies are a valuable tool. The motivational treasure box is within your building; we must be confident enough to acknowledge that we would like to upgrade the perspectives in our area of expertise. This adjustment is not about admitting that we are less of an instructor, less of a barista; it is admitting we are prioritizing learning above our own pride. Admirable.

THE FOCUSED HANDS: OWN YOUR NAVIGATION

Although we realize that our skill set comes second to our will set, we also realize that our lack of aptitude in a certain area could stymie our instructional practice or interest in the course material. In times like these, it is quite okay to be humble and admit it is possible when we "know we do not know" and then look to do something about it.

Students appreciate when you can bring something fresh, current, and fascinating to the classroom and diminish their perception that school is boring. And how can we make life for anyone less boring? Nick would say it is a matter of swapping shoes with the "team members," or employees. "I got into this business because I want to make a difference in this world. When I was 22, and fresh out of college, I realized if I want to make a difference in scale, in business, it's going to take me a long time to climb the ladder and get to a place where I can make decisions that matter or make a difference in people's lives, or I could just start a business that is going to be predicated on making a difference in people's lives. And that's what I chose to do. So everything I've done at Saxbys is to literally put myself in that person's shoes and say, '**would I want to do this job?**' Like, when I was in college would I want to have a barista job? In effect, wear the shoes of your students and ask if they would want to teach your class. Wear the shoes of your employees and ask if they would want to run your department or your company."

There is a direct correlation with the relationships we build with students (clients/guests) to their desire to learn and attend class (work). Building relationships takes time and small conversations in the hall, in between classes, and while checking homework afford pockets of time to make connections. Implementing mini life lessons into our classes might be a deeper way to not only connect with the hearts of our students but to raise the level of interest and engagement in our job. To avoid the excuse "I don't have time," don't be regimented about these lessons; it adds undue pressure. Seize the life lesson moments more spontaneously like when you finish a lesson early, you have five minutes before a pre-scheduled fire drill, or you are waiting to be called to an assembly. Let the lessons be their own surprise for you and for the students.

How often do you play music while you are working? Some teachers have begun implementing meditation and yoga into their classes as a means to center the students and aid in their focus. Consider getting out the markers, crayons, and colored pencils. Take notes on drawing paper instead of on notebook paper. Imagine employees gathering for a staff meeting to find markers, crayons, and poster board instead of laptops and a projected media presentation. Any medium that adds a new flare engages you and enlivens your approach. Experience and navigate new avenues of presentation methods; you are in control of how you deliver content to students and employees and how you offer ideas to them.

Don't settle into being a prisoner of routine in your school or in the workplace. That is a perception that we create and we must evolve from that. Being stuck in a rut is an emotional choice that we make because the actions in our day are not igniting the spirit of who we are. Chances are they are not igniting our students, coworkers, or colleagues either.

In the business realm, consider Nick's words in that "our business stands for so much more than serving coffee. It's a vehicle for education and opportunity, it's exciting." Our goal is to make each venture for a customer or student exciting and worthwhile. It's not really work if we enjoy what we are doing; and the enjoyment we can gain out of serving others with a passion and purpose will make any Saxbys glass overflow. Time to get brewing!

NOTE

1. All Nick Bayer quotes presented in this chapter are from an in-person interview with the authors that took place on June 14, 2018.

19

We're Talking about Connections, Man! I Mean How Silly Is That? We're Talking about Connections!

Connect and Cultivate

> Sometimes we walk around not even knowing how much we know, or how much we have to offer until we are faced with, or offered an opportunity to help someone else. That's the beauty of it; we can put our talents to use for those that really need it.
>
> —Chris Franklin, *chairman and CEO, Aqua America*
> with Nick DeBenedictis, *former chairman and CEO;*
> *current board member, Aqua America*[1]

Have you ever considered the power of changing a child through changing or influencing a parent? In the educational field, we develop relationships with parents with the intention of parent confidence. Our ability to build bridges with parents begins with the first encounter and grows through genuine, inclusive communication that cultivates a relationship of trust. Our objective is to maintain concurrent instruction and construction, reaching the parents and the students, creating trustworthy relationships that benefit all involved.

The same holds true for the folks outside of the educational field per se. In other words, we all have an opportunity to impact children (and others) throughout our days if we desire to witness the opportunities that present themselves. Chris Franklin, CEO of Aqua America, witnesses his (and his company's) power within the communities in which they serve.

Chris sees three critical aspects to the idea of philanthropy. In his words, it's not just about writing a check that matters:

> We're trying to connect three elements with that (philanthropic) work. The first one, we put aside some philanthropic dollars at the company in our foundation every year and we put those dollars aside to help nonprofit charitable organizations. It's one thing to just say, "hey, listen you're a great organization, let me write you a check, congratulations,

keep doing your good work." But what we're trying to do with this program is we're trying to say, here's some philanthropic dollars but we also have talent in our company.

Whether it's engineering, or accounting, or the various people who do things with their hands, plumbing, pipe connecting or chemists; we're trying to connect our philanthropic dollars with our talents through volunteerism. We demonstrated this work even beyond the areas where we serve water. In fact, we've had employees travel to Nicaragua and Panama to help solve community water issues. The third element, in addition to philanthropic dollars and volunteerism is camaraderie. What we are trying to do is say, hey, we will sponsor and then we will provide volunteers and by the way, Aqua employees, we want you to do it with a minimum of ten employees because the ulterior motive there is to build team spirit, to build camaraderie inside the company.

So, we take all three elements of our foundation dollars, our volunteerism, and our building of camaraderie, and we try to tie them all together to accomplish the overall goal of doing good things for the community, building goodwill in the community and investing in the community through our corporate dollars, and building team spirit inside the company.

In reviewing the central message in Chris's words, the pathway to cultivating relationships with people entails constructing trust, constructing communication, and constructing capacity and potential. If we can balance genuine, energized efforts that relate to people's needs, then our role as a "giver" becomes more enjoyable, fulfilling, and effective.

> *And so far it has worked really, really well we are very pleased; and the Villanova project* (Villanova students and Aqua employees collaborated in Panama and Nicaragua to solve water-related problems and also donate time and goods to the local people) *is just one example but we're doing similar work throughout the company—in Texas and in North Carolina, and in Pennsylvania, we do it with stream cleanups, we do it with all sorts of things, and it is really meant to draw in environmental organizations and other nonprofits and to not only invest in them but to make them believers in Aqua being a good company.*

Too often, we can and do use the convenient out when it comes to money. Like Chris alluded to, it is too easy to just hand over the check instead of our hands in the process of giving.

In schools, this thought process can play out in various ways. For example, have you ever considered what parents want for their children? In countless reads and conversations, we have come across descriptors to complete the statement, *I want my children to be* . . . responsible, honest, kind-hearted, hard-working, successful, organized, reliable, dependable, and humble. Meanwhile, kids care mostly about being independent, left alone, and happy. Parents focus on the larger picture traits and values while students focus on the in-the-moment traits. Students know that someday they need to be decisive, but right now, they want to be funny, tired, sad, and so on.

When you develop relationships with parents and students, the challenge is not only the varied desires of each but the recognition that each is in a different season of life. Parents don't want their kids to grow up too fast, but they sure would love if the kids acquired adult traits at a young age! As teachers, we need to help both students and parents feel empowered and establish a relationship with both headed in the same direction. And we do this by focusing on not only the core content (the given, the money), but the whole child as well.

As we have mentioned before, positive influence is contagious. And it was easy to see that Chris Franklin's core mission was very similar to Nick DeBenedictis' (former CEO of Aqua America) high standards. In alignment with Chris's initial change, Nick believed (and still does) that Aqua's "over all driving mission is to improve the quality of life of the people in the greater Philadelphia area in the twentieth century and now in the twenty first century across the eight states we serve."

In schools or business, each has an identity that the greater public visualizes when they think of the entity. We call it branding. This type of recognition is critical for both the bottom line, but also the human component of why we do what we do. Nick spoke to us about this commitment, and he believed that name recognition was vitally important to the overall health of both the organization's internal and external publics:

> (Philanthropy—having a positive impact on human beings) puts a face on the company. Anything that brings disciplines together for a non-work related atmosphere helps build relationships within the company. It's got to be a part of your culture that giving back to the community is really important.
>
> Clearly there is an enlightened self-interest. We are a regulated for-profit company; we serve the people who talk to the same legislators and regulators. So, there is blatant self-interest. But, I call it enlightened self-interest because it helps, not only does it help our bottom line, but it helps the people that we are serving to want to help us be profitable. (Nick DeBenedictis)

In Nick's tenure, and now in Chris's, we can attest to Aqua's success both in the market place and in our communities. The key is transparency. Make no mistake—all of these companies desire to make money; but what they do with that profit, the impact they have on the greater good, genuinely allows for the sustainability of the company's success. In simple terms, we realize Aqua is making a profit, but when we witness the good they are doing in our communities, we can reconcile in our brains the positive force that they have become.

As Chris referenced so eloquently, "At the very most basic level, (Aqua America) needs to be involved in the communities because this is where we are anchored and where we have been for 130 years and will probably, hopefully, be for another 130 years. That's very basic but more importantly than that, I believe the vast number of people that work in our company believe that we have a responsibility to the communities where we serve."

In schools, that same transparency is critical for our own sustained success. In other words, teaching is "good for us." We do indeed get a ton out of being that critical factor in a child's life, and there are many times when our influence becomes the force that sets a child on the right path. Yet, we must always remember that families are seeking their moments as well. In other words, parental involvement is beneficial for teachers, but it is especially beneficial for their children. When kids see that their parents are personally invested in the school community, the students are more motivated, they have improved behavior, they enjoy attending school, and their overall outlook is positive and hopeful. Our role is to encourage parental involvement for the best interest of the students.

The pathway to cultivating relationships with parents entails constructing trust, constructing communication, and constructing capacity and potential. If we can balance genuine, energized instruction that relates to students with the construction of a trusted, honest relationship with parents, then our role as a teacher becomes more enjoyable, fulfilling, and effective.

To construct capacity and potentiality with parents, we must help parents see that they have the potential within themselves to give their kids courage and a strong self-esteem. Inspire parents to raise their kids to be originals and focus on them as individuals. Through the vehicle of communication we choose, throw in some parenting advice that is encouraging, reminding parents that what they are experiencing is all part of the journey. Provide them with confidence to be a relational parent who loves their kids for who they are and who raises them based on their own strengths. Parents need to know that mistakes do not define their kids; they are defined by the heart of who they are.

Here is where the merge of business and schools occurs. Involvement! Just as Nick and Chris know the greatest type of giving involves the hands (not just the dollars), we (in education) must realize and encourage others to be a "part of the process." It is one thing for a parent to go to her child's games and quite another to coach. But times are tough with family work schedules. We know; therefore, we must try to break down experiences so that families can fit their limited time into a meaningful activity or experience with their children to build connectedness and trust. For instance, although at the elementary level family involvement is "more welcome" from staff and students, perhaps a different type of involvement could be present at the higher grades. Career days and field chaperones are all ways that parents can do something small which could have a big impact on relaying to children that mom or dad is still here, still involved.

The key here is to continue to keep the dialogues open between families and ourselves, families, and each other. Chris talked about balance when we discussed what made for a connected Aqua employee: "And so we are starting to really be conscious of, if we can help people balance their work and their personal life, you tend to have a happier employee, you tend to have people who feel more trusted, more empowered so we are spending a lot of time thinking and trying new ideas around this. I think it's critically important."

In schools, and business, we believe that this balance can occur when we first open the lines of communication to ultimately understand the needs of each other. Reaching a place where each of us is looking out for the best interest of the individuals collectively will serve both fronts well.

THE FOCUSED HANDS: OWN YOUR CONNECTIONS

Chris was amazing with one of his final thoughts which helps to summarize not only this chapter, but all the chapters. He stated, "At the end of the day we're all human beings. We want to be motivated, we want to be cared for, we want to feel valued. These are all necessary things in our life and whether we're at home or at work or at school, a lot of the same needs have to be met."

So true! We all have needs. We all have that desire for connection, for companionship, for love. Be it in the workplace or classroom, our ability to give of ourselves, through our hands and words, ultimately provides the foundation for sustainability and success.

For educators, consider that the power of influencing a parent could be the power that changes a child. Consider how you reach out to parents; how would your role change if you had a greater percentage of empowered parents? Design a vehicle of communication that is going to reach parents more regularly and more positively, one that is going to make parents feel like you have opened a door for a relationship with them. Be excited to engage with parents and get to know them because you have the same goal in mind—a dedicated, independent, happy person.

For business folks, consider how your words and actions not only sustain your happiness, but also the person impacted by your actions and the company as a whole. In Chris's words, "If we start the discussion at our companies and with our students about honesty and integrity, start there, it's really the basis for so many other things, and then build upon that with excellence. I think greatness can come out of it because people feel challenged and empowered and they can really rise to the occasion." That could not have been said better.

NOTES

1. All Chris Franklin quotes presented in this chapter are from a phone interview with the authors that took place on June 12, 2018.
2. All Nick DeBenedictis quotes presented in this chapter are from a phone interview with the authors that took place on July 12, 2018.

20

What If You Were Paid to Sell the Greatness of Your Workplace? Would You Be a Millionaire?

Brand and Promote

> People reach out to understand how we incorporate kindness into our culture and understand the importance of, particularly now in today's world, the importance of being more than just a business, more than just a growth engine.
>
> —John Leahy, *former president and COO, KIND Healthy Snacks*[1]

When thinking about branding, we were instantly drawn to John Leahy and KIND. One of the basic premises to branding is simplicity of the mission. In other words, consult established marketing companies, and they will tell you that the more often a simple message gets promoted, the more recognizable it becomes to the consumer. Furthermore, the more that message establishes a positive tone, the more likely folks are to think fondly of both the product and the company. And for our purposes, what message could be better than that of KIND?

As John Leahy, president of KIND, indicates, "Everything we do centers around doing the KIND thing for your body, your taste buds, and your world. It works because all of our products are KIND, with a nutrient dense first ingredient. And our social mission is called the KIND Movement and we also operate The KIND Foundation. It all ties together which is a real benefit in the way that it's been built."

This type of philosophy permeates in both business and schools. Being a positive voice for your school markets its greatness and conveys a depiction of the students and staff through prideful storytelling and highlights of achievements. **We are not only a member of our school; We are a reflection of its products: the students.** When we speak highly of our school, we show our belief in its potential and we show our commitment to its effectiveness as a learning institution for students. By marketing our school, we are illuminating the excellence of our colleagues, the administration, the families, and the community.

It's never too late to adopt a positive outlook on your school (your place of business) and share it out with others. All schools go through changes and experience growth in different ways. Sometimes the change is challenging, even stressful. Sometimes the change makes us doubt the good that is allegedly on the other side. The more we can occupy our attitude with the positive qualities, regardless of our opinion of the transition, the more likely we will ignite ourselves as positive people.

When you believe it, you become it.

Believing in the power of our school evokes a powerful image of ourselves. We proudly tell people that our staff is amazing, knowing that we are subtly saying that we are amazing . . . because we are. Be proud of being a piece of the puzzle that creates an outstanding school.

This message is echoed at KIND. In a great story John told, the basis for this type of *believe it, be it* resounds through its message:

I thought I was pretty good at kindness, third from the bottom, raised in a great value system, my father was a naval academy graduate, my mother was an all American hockey player at Trinity in DC. I thought I was pretty good until I started to work here. And then I realized, in my own life that I can be kinder, and I can be more forgiving, and I can be patient. I wear KIND gear and I travel all around the country—you know what airport lines are like, and the frustration of traveling. Guess what? **When you have that KIND logo on, you better check yourself, you better check your ego at security. Kindness becomes more top-of-mind, it grows on you.**

In the past we've celebrated KIND Causes or socially-impactful organizations. We've also celebrated KIND People transforming their communities through kindness. One winner took over all of these old city buses and turned them into showers and sinks for the homeless in San Francisco. With our funding, she was able to roll it out to other markets, like LA. Another individual was providing water in the suburbs of Detroit. We had these KIND People come to our company meeting and talk about their work and give our team members a chance to get involved. We embed kindness into our culture, so it's not just something we do behind the scenes.

This is one of John's stories of unbridled empathy when it comes to the connection of company and compassion. **When you look at your life story, and how you have authored it, is it inspirational?** Is it something you can brand and promote? When you teach students, you don't wait until the perfect student enters your room to be the best teacher you can be, you don't wait until the perfect classroom gets constructed to be the best teacher you can be, and you don't wait until they hire the perfect principal to be the best teacher you can be. But, in our personal lives, many of us wait until that *something* comes along so we can be the best person we can be. We wait for the perfect time in life or we wait until our kids are a certain age or we just simply settle to say, "I will do that when . . ."

If there is anything commanding about chapters 1 through 20, it is this: **stop waiting.** Start living your life as the teacher and the person you know you can be. The weight of time continues to press on everyone; when you value the brevity of time, you begin to live with an underlying fire that keeps igniting you and fueling you forward. The *grain of salt* (and that's a generous portion, mathematically speaking) life you have is limited by an undefined end; that, in and of itself, is the motivating factor for everything you do and every feeling you embrace.

Commit to branding and promoting your school and yourself, not with arrogance but with confidence and a sense of pride. Your positivity about life and work will elevate; you will feel more empowered to get involved and be more enthusiastic. Only good can come of that perspective. Imagine the alternative. You probably know people who exhibit the alternative. Where is it getting them? Would you say that they are maximizing their life? Likely not, in fact, you might even say they are minimizing their life or wasting it. If you first get inspired and are confident with who you are, your fire can ignite others and you can create a workplace where the greater percentage of the staff knows the value of a maximized life.

Students in the classrooms want to have teachers who love their school, who know that it is a great, productive, safe, and invigorating learning institution. Students don't want teachers who are gloomy or who are negative about their environment. Your attitude toward your school is a convincing one, and it should be contagious. If the students know you love the school, they will also begin to seek reasons to love the school. Imagine teaching in a place where the students love the school! It is within your realm to promote that sentiment.

When speaking with John, you can just get a sense that he lives the tenets of this chapter. He does not only talk the talk but walks the walk in his words and his actions:

I love KIND. People love our products. And like I said, it starts with the products, I mean we are a company that gives back but we also want to be economically sustainable. All team members carry these #kindawesome cards. If I see someone give up their seat on the train (I commute in from Connecticut) to someone who is elderly or someone who is pregnant or someone who has little children, I will go over to them and say, that was really kind of you. I'd like to offer you a #kindawesome card. If I have a product I will give them the product too. It's a way to celebrate people for their kindness. Recipients can go online and we will send them more #kindawesome cards so that they can spread kindness in their own lives, along with a complementary KIND bar. It's a simple way to introduce people to our mission and our products simultaneously.

THE FOCUSED HANDS: OWN YOUR BRANDING

When you are out in the community, make a concerted effort to brand and promote your entity. Stay in touch with your school or business through the newsletters, online articles, and sponsored events. Recommit yourself to only speak positively about your role at your business, the service you render, and the people you serve.

Be complimentary of your colleagues for their successes; yes this requires a bit of humility. Magnify the strengths of the staff and the company and you will find you also magnify yourself.

If you have not already witnessed, branding defines culture. It is the lifeline to the consumer and the people of the company. That connection is required to enhance not only the reputation, but the actual bottom line for charity (which ultimately serves the bottom line). In John's final words, he stated that one of the things that is really cool about KIND is the culture. People want to be here. They celebrate our social mission and live our KIND values. Every year, we shut down the whole company and our team members across the country do a day of service. We visit soup kitchens, we are in parks digging dirt, putting mulch. Daniel (Daniel Lubetzky, CEO and Founder) and I hit usually four or five sites in New York City. I don't look good in a hair net, but when I'm serving people at a food pantry, I'll gladly wear one.

Team members appreciate the mission, but they are equally committed to building our business. They operate with an ownership attitude and demonstrate a commitment to excellence every day. Everyone has an opportunity to grow their careers here—to be part of this exciting journey. I can't wait to see what we accomplish next.

KIND is not just a snack; it's a mindset. What's yours?

NOTE

1. All John Leahy quotes presented in this chapter are from an in-person interview with the authors that took place on June 20, 2018.

21

Examine Your Enthusiasm for Life, Hope You Don't Need a Microscope!

Ignite Hearts

> What do you want people to remember about you after they've met you for the first time? I call this your "instant legacy." Here resides a singular moment comprised of your capacity to impact another person; what you choose to do with that moment (is your choice).
>
> —Andrew Stine, *teacher, Twin Valley Middle School*[1]

Throughout this text, we have tried to make connections between the corporate world and schools. We have primarily focused on the words of advice from our CEO friends to identify many of the traits that not only made them (and their entities) pronounced, but also the impact of the business on the employees, customers, and society at large.

In this last chapter, our focus switches a bit, as we conclude with a classroom CEO, Mr. Andrew Stine. Andrew is a teacher at Twin Valley Middle School, and truthfully, he is one of the most amazing teachers we have ever met. Andrew has a zest and passion that is completely unmatched, as his love for his students, families, colleagues, and the school as a whole is apparent through his actions and, of course, his words.

When asked about concluding our book, Andrew, being the modest man that he is, was not only humbled, but also felt a sense of responsibility in this charge. You see, Andrew's creed in his classroom is to "teach life" to all students because they all deserve it. We call this his personal priority. Much like all of the CEOs we have mentioned, Andrew also believes that the only true way to impact another human being is by marrying the mind, heart, and hands. Within his words, we have found this central message to ring clear and true.

As in the initial quote from this chapter, Andrew believes that we "set the tone for our legacy" when we initially meet. As he stated in our discussion, "When I meet someone for the first time, and maybe the only time, I want them to remember that I was genuinely positive, and that I made their time with me enjoyable. This applies in every situation I find myself in. Whether it is passing someone in an aisle in the grocery store for less than thirty seconds, spending a weekend with a best friend, or working with students in my classroom all year. I work hard at making sure people have a good time when I am around. I believe in this because optimism and positivity are strong forces that can change the world."

Hopefully, from this short quote, you can get a sense of the positive energy and magnetism Andrew carries. It truly is remarkable. We believe that this energy gets its source from having a passion for life. As Andrew believes, "To me, life is fun. Life is a good time. It is more than the daily grind and the monotonous nature of humankind. Life is a gift that presents us with unique opportunities to decide what we'll do with it. This is best summed up by an expression my friends and I use often: 'Live your life.' It encourages us to be in the moment rather than miss opportunities and live with regrets. Worrying about the struggles of life will not make any progress since worrying stifles positivity.

It is often said that life is short. If life is so short and we're always in a race against the clock, and if we always say, 'I wish we had more time,' why wouldn't we want to be enthusiastic about every minute of the day? Why wouldn't we want to share that passion and that energy with everyone? This conscious awareness of joyfully living in the present drives me to be better, happier, and more energetic in all aspects of my life.

People feel joy from making others happy. This is universal. Humans get a selfish reward for being selfless in their service unto others. That is why I do what I do as a sibling, as a friend, and as a teacher. I get a good feeling from helping others to have that same feeling. I'm motivated to make my own life and the lives of others exceptional. This is not to say that life is always perfect, we all have struggles in life and constant ups and downs. When we interact with others for the first time, however, they don't know what struggles we're having so we must do our best not to allow those difficulties to affect our mission or taint our last impression."

By now, you are probably saying, "Shouldn't he be writing this book?" Truth be told, he could, hence why we chose him to close. You see, words are powerful, as represented in each chapter, as captured by the title. What we say matters! **Words reveal the labors of the mind, heart, and hands; therefore, we must choose them wisely.**

Gone are the days when we can simply toss out a simple phrase or the latest jargon and expect people to respond to us as if we truly care about them. People are much more sophisticated than that. People do indeed hear our words, and they judge us by them, especially when we first meet, which is why teachers and people in service carry such a heavy burden of setting a positive tone from Jump Street.

Andrew has an interesting hobby when it comes to this topic. He explains that "one of my favorite things to do is to hold conversations with complete strangers. 'But people don't like to be bothered,' my critics would say. They would be surprised to hear, however, that in most cases strangers are receptive to having meaningful conversations. To be clear, these conversations go beyond the typical discussion about weather or traffic. Small talk is too predictable for me and for the other person. There is no chance for me to make a meaningful impact if I am an ordinary stranger talking about ordinary things. If I truly want to leave a positive instant legacy, I need to skip the small talk and jump in with something unexpected. For me, it is fun to say to myself, 'I'm going up to that person to make their day.'"

Here is an example of something I've used before as a starter: "Excuse me. You look highly qualified, and I could use your help. I have a hypothetical scenario for you, and I'd like your opinion. If the world was going to end tomorrow, and you were chosen to select the artist that will headline the last concert on earth, which artist, living or deceased, would you pick?"

There are many things I like about this question, but one reason is that it references a universal language; music. It offers something that everyone can relate to. This type of question is low-stress for the other person and gives them a fun brain break. At times, this has even led to a long, but meaningful explanation as to why they answered the way they did. To this day, I've never been disappointed by an answer because it almost always leads to further dialogue. Afterward, I can walk away and know that the two minutes we spoke gave them a positive moment in their life. Again, I've now left my "instant legacy."

How can we not be inspired by such bold thoughts as to be the brightest spot of someone's day!

Too often, in business and schools, we focus on the product instead of the person. And although we have goals to attain, scores to be reached, we need to adjust our words to first start with the human being in front of us rather than the product. For teachers, this can be a tall order, as the pressure to cover the standards is immense. As Andrew expressed,

> As teachers, we must be flexible. Yes, we have to teach the content and curriculum assigned to us. But no one says we can't go beyond that.
>
> I believe it is our duty to go beyond the curriculum, to seek out those teachable moments and to share our passion for learning. This is much easier said than done, however, and we must be ready to revive our own passion. Passion is extremely critical to the overall success of a teacher. I find that teachers too often lose the passion that they once had. So many state and federal regulations, additional responsibilities, and larger class sizes weigh teachers down. We must not forget our purpose and what drives our passion. For me, I remind myself daily that I am shaping a human life. I am impacting a human being.
>
> I became a teacher because I wanted to be a child's champion. I wanted to make improvements in the education system. I felt, and still feel strongly, that becoming a lifelong learner is a key to a successful life. When an educator deeply thinks about the influence they have on a developing life, they realize the importance of their position. An educator's purpose is clear and consequences are obvious. We impact the future.

This same philosophy holds true for Ed Herr, or Marcus Allen, or Phil Martelli, or you and me. The manner in which we "go beyond" what is expected sets the mark for an entirely different experience, one that is filled with unexpected joy and passion. These are the moments that all human beings crave—the opportunity to be noticed as a person who matters, who is respected and capable of being more than just the title below their name indicates.

Here, we desire the connection; and we long for the moment when all three pillars (mind, heart, and hands) align. Remember, one of the most impactful ways we can build a bridge to security is by first engaging in a meaningful, connected conversation. As is evidenced with Andrew's perspective, the first words could be the most lasting ones to a person's ears—if and only if we initiate the connection.

THE FOCUSED HANDS: OWN YOUR WORDS

As human beings, we are constantly learning, constantly taking in knowledge through our senses to make meaning from the world. One sure fire way to ignite this process is to see ourselves (CEO or employee) as beacons of learning through a happy disposition. In Andrew's words,

> Learning is just as fun as life itself. I make being happy a priority, and I make my students' happiness a priority. I leave every class with a story to tell someone else. I want them to say, 'Guess what Mr. Stine did/said today?!' Why do I do all of these things? I do these things to grab their attention and to make them laugh. I know that not every student loves school and learning, but I also know that every student does love to smile and laugh. I do this because I know that when students are more engaged, they are more likely to understand the content being taught. If I can give a student joy and happiness and teach them something new, then I can be satisfied with my day's work. I also do these things because I know I need to be the best for my students. They deserve my best and nothing less. They deserve someone who will make every interaction a positive one and show unwavering care and attention.
>
> Education's ultimate goal is to produce successful functioning members of society. But we do not need to settle for producing average individuals. Let's make members of society who are above average and have a passion that cannot be stopped. Teachers should cultivate this culture in their classrooms and the end result will be students who look back at their time in the school and think about the fun they had while learning new things. Start each school year and each work day, no matter what your job is, with a drive to create positive interactions and amazing first impressions. Be a champion for everyone you meet. Be someone who makes others smile and happy. Be passionate about life, not just certain aspects of it.

As we turn the page from this chapter, promise yourself that you will put this book down and go directly to the person nearest you and engage in some type of meaningful dialogue. Promise yourself you will do this with a positive spirit, and we promise you, you will not be disappointed.

NOTE

1. All Andrew Stine quotes presented in this chapter are from an in-person interview with the authors that took place on February 26, 2018.

About the Editors

Joy Rosser has been a teacher since 1995, serving students and families in the suburban districts of Philadelphia. Beyond the classroom walls, her passions are ignited by family, friends, professional boards, presentations, writing, and an ongoing canine climate at home!

Anthony Barber's reality is education. As the superintendent of a growing suburban school just outside of Philadelphia, he is in constant contact with teachers, staff, students, families, and businesses facing the very issues in this text. Anthony has taught at several universities instructing graduate courses for potential superintendents, principals, and teachers.

Before they were even in middle school, Joy and Tony connected on the court in the Ridley, Pennsylvania, ABA recreational basketball program. Basketball practices and tournaments instilled competitiveness, collaboration, and a spirit for success—with a taste of failure, too. Hours of gym and travel time with their families set the foundation for a cherished friendship while competing in a sport they both loved. However, as such is the case with many childhood sports stories, they gradually lost contact with one another as they set out on separate paths to pursue their goals.

Fast-forward thirty-five years . . .

Joy and Tony, during a chance school visit, reconnected, and began to reminisce about the old times. Ironically, both of them had found their way into educational careers. With a shared, continuous passion to compete and learn, they agreed to stay in contact with one another and perhaps work as a team together someday . . . little did they know that this text would be the result of such a promise.

About the Contributors

Marcus Allen (chapter 9) is the CEO of the Greater Philadelphia region's largest and most experienced youth mentoring organization—celebrated its 100th anniversary in 2015. In April of 2013, Allen became the first African American CEO of Big Brothers Big Sisters Independence Region's (BBBS IR) celebrated history. For three consecutive years, he has significantly grown the Agency as measured by the number of children served, revenue generation from donors and programs, and overall visibility. This impressive growth garnered BBBS IR a "Gold Standard Award" in 2013 and the coveted "Pinnacle Award" in 2014 from BBBS America, given to only four affiliates of the 334 affiliated agencies across the country. Prior to joining BBBS IR, Allen was President/CEO of ACHIEVEability.

Nick Bayer (chapter 18) has always been in the business of bringing people together, whether it's as one of *Philadelphia Business Journal's* "Most Admired CEO," or as a consummate team captain since Little League. So when he created Saxbys in 2005, Nick never really considered it to be a coffee company—instead, it's a social impact company fueled by amazing food, beverage, and hospitality. Saxbys has since grown from one corner café to a thirty-unit, Philadelphia-based business with a singular mission: Make Life Better.

Pete Ciarrocchi (chapter 7) is the chairman and CEO of Chickie's & Pete's Crab House and Sports Bar, an expanding chain of restaurants that has become part of the true fabric of the city of Philadelphia and an avid sports fan's "must stop" before, during, or after the game.

About the Contributors

Bernard Dagenais (chapter 10) is the president and CEO of The Main Line Chamber of Commerce, which looks out for the interests of member businesses throughout Southeastern Pennsylvania. He spent twenty-seven years as a journalist for news organizations in Vermont, Washington, DC, and Philadelphia.

Nick DeBenedictis (chapter 19) is a member of the board of directors of Aqua America. He previously served as chairman and CEO of Aqua from June 1993 to July 2015. Aqua America is a publicly traded water and wastewater utility holding company with operating subsidiaries that serve about three million people in eight states.

Chris Franklin (chapter 19) is the chairman and CEO of Aqua America, a 133-year-old regulated water and wastewater utility with roots in southeastern Pennsylvania. Chris is celebrating twenty-five years with Aqua, where he previously served in public affairs and investor relations, customer operations, and as COO. His industry leadership extends to his service as president of the National Association of Water Companies board of directors.

Chris Gheysens (chapter 11) is the president and CEO of Wawa, a chain of more than 800 convenience stores located in six states and known for their fresh food and award-winning coffee. Wawa is a family- and associate-owned, privately held company. Approximately 32,000 associates provide convenient, friendly, and inviting experiences for over 1.6 million customers every day.

Andrea Gilbert (chapter 6) joined Main Line Health in June 2000 as the senior vice president of Bryn Mawr Hospital. She was named president of Bryn Mawr Hospital in 2002. During Ms. Gilbert's tenure, Bryn Mawr Hospital has earned the distinction as a top 100 Hospital in the nation in 2011 and 2009 by the Thomson Reuters Organization and had consistently ranked among the Philadelphia region's best hospitals in *US News & World Report* since 2011. Bryn Mawr Hospital was ranked #1 in the *Philadelphia Business Journal*'s Best Places to Work in 2005. Ms. Gilbert has more than thirty years of experience in health care and hospital administration, including positions at the Department of Health, Education, and Welfare in Washington,

DC; the Inova Health System in Falls Church, Virginia; and the Allegheny and Tenet Health Systems, Philadelphia. Before joining Bryn Mawr Hospital, Ms. Gilbert was the CEO at City Avenue Hospital in Philadelphia. Ms. Gilbert is a graduate of the University of Wisconsin and holds a master's degree in health administration and planning from Johns Hopkins University.

Nicholas (Nick) J. Giuffre (chapter 15) is the former president and CEO of Bradford White Corporation and its subsidiaries, one of the most technologically advanced manufacturers of water heating, space heating, combination heating, and water storage products in the world. He joined the company in 1978 following his graduation from Bloomsburg University, where he earned a bachelor of science degree in business management.

H. Edward Hanway (chapter 2) is the former chairman and CEO of Cigna Corporation and now serves as the nonexecutive chairman of Marsh & McLennan Companies, Inc. He currently serves as the chairman of Faith in the Future, an independent foundation that provides strategic management and operational oversight of seventeen high schools and four schools of special education in the Archdiocese of Philadelphia, and provides support services to all Archdiocesan schools in the five county Philadelphia areas. A member of the Pennsylvania and American Institutes of Certified Public Accountants, Hanway graduated from Loyola College of Baltimore (BA, 1974) and Widener University (MBA, 1984).

Ed Herr (chapter 3) grew up working in his family's snack food business. As president of Herr Foods Incorporated, Ed is committed to upholding the Herr Family tradition of offering customers the very best products and service in the industry, all from a company that cultivates a spirit of teamwork and appreciation for every individual. He is a director of several local non-profit organizations, including the Lighthouse Youth Center, Oxford Senior Center, and Oxford Mainstreet, Inc. He is a founding member and director of SILO (Serving, Inspiring, and Loving Others), based in Oxford, Pennsylvania. Ed also serves as a director of New York City Relief (NYCR) and the Council of the Navigators Church Discipleship Ministry, based in Colorado Springs.

After a seventeen-year distinguished career as an NFL quarterback, today **Ron Jaworski** (foreword) is coaching football fans on TV. Before switching to his current multiplatform analyst role with ESPN, Ron spent five seasons in the booth with Mike Tirico and Jon Gruden as the color commentator for *Monday Night Football*. He also owns an exclusive  business development company called *Business Clubs America*, in addition to six signature golf courses in the Greater Philadelphia Area. Jaworski also serves as co-majority owner of the Philadelphia Soul, chairman of the Board of NFL Alumni Association, and sits on the boards of PNC Bank.

A graduate of LaSalle University, **Gary Jonas Jr.** (chapter 5) began his career in real estate by learning the mortgage business, while refining the art of structuring. Jonas joined forces with two colleagues to establish Advanced Mortgage Concepts, where he served as president for ten years. While overseeing the activities and growth of Advanced Mortgage Concepts, Jonas began a quest to revitalize blighted properties in the city of Philadelphia—where he was born, bred, and educated. This venture rapidly grew into The HOW Group, a highly respected real estate firm that focuses primarily on urban real estate development/acquisitions, construction, property management, real estate, and lending. As president of The HOW Group, Jonas focuses primarily on the acquisitions and development activities, and hires top-notch personnel partners to handle the operations.

John Leahy (chapter 20) is the former president and COO of KIND Healthy Snacks, a brand of nutritious and delicious snacks made from premium ingredient, like nuts, seeds, whole grains, and fruit. John has more than thirty years of experience in consumer products, holding titles of escalating responsibility, from district sales manager, to president at prestigious CPG companies including NBTY and Playtex. John holds a BS degree from Villanova University and resides in Huntington, Connecticut, with his wife, Ann. He also has three children: John David, Bridget, and Devon. To give back, John guest-lectures at St. Joseph's University and Villanova University every semester in both their undergraduate and master's program.

William (Bill) J. Marrazzo (chapter 13) currently serves as the president and CEO of WHYY, Inc., the leading public media organization serving southeastern Pennsylvania, southern New Jersey, and all of Delaware. Leading the development of new digital technologies at WHYY, Bill has ushered in an evolving number of video, audio, and web distribution pathways, enabling WHYY to systematically grow its ranking within one of the nation's largest and most complex media markets. Before joining WHYY in November 1997, Bill's career included senior executive roles in the environmental and water industries. Bill earned a bachelor's degree in chemical engineering at the University of Delaware, and he completed graduate course work for a master's in chemical engineering at Villanova University.

About the Contributors

Phil Martelli (chapter 17) coached twenty-four seasons as the head men's basketball coach at Saint Joseph's University, having built a program that is consistently one of the top in the conference, a perennial post-season participant, and a key player on the national scene. One of the more respected coaches in the game, he is the Hawks' all-time leader in career victories. Martelli has taken his team to the NCAA Tournament thirteen times, including the Elite Eight in 2004, and has led SJU to three Atlantic 10 Conference championships.

PHIL MARTELLI
Saint Joseph's Basketball

Thomas Mehler (chapter 14) is the president of Southco, Inc. Thomas began his journey in technical sales before holding numerous leadership positions in sales, operations, business unit management, and general management. Before moving to the United States, Thomas lived in Europe and Asia, while leading and overseeing Southco's expansion into these Key Growth Regions. Southco is the global leader in engineered Industrial Access Hardware and supplies products to many Fortune 500 companies in industries such as automotive, aerospace, medical, electronics, and telecom.

Denis P. O'Brien (chapter 12) is the senior executive vice president of Exelon: Baltimore Gas & Electric (BGE), Commonwealth Edison Company (ComEd), and PECO. The company is the largest regulated electric and natural gas delivery company in the United States. O'Brien previously served as executive vice president of Exelon and CEO of Philadelphia-based PECO. He serves on the board of Independence Blue Cross, and on numerous civic and industry boards, including the CEO of Council for Growth and the Franklin Institute. He is a former chair of the Greater Philadelphia Chamber of Commerce and the Edison Electric Power Research Institute (EPRI), and a former board member of the Pennsylvania Business Council, among others. O'Brien holds a bachelor's degree in industrial engineering from Rutgers University and earned a master's degree in business from Drexel University.

Angelo R. Perryman (chapter 8) is second-generation president and CEO of Perryman Building and Construction Services Inc., a commercial general construction and construction management services firm with headquarters in Philadelphia, Pennsylvania. Perryman Construction has completed over 1,000 projects and is also an active sponsor and participant in numerous community and civic endeavors in its current home base, the Mid-Atlantic region.

About the Contributors

Kevin Reilly (chapter 16) was born in Wilmington, Delaware. While at Villanova University, Kevin was voted the team's MVP and first team All-East linebacker. In 1973, the World Champion Miami Dolphins drafted Kevin in the seventh round. Later that year, he returned to his hometown team of the Philadelphia Eagles, serving as captain of the special teams. After retiring from the NFL, Kevin worked as a senior executive in sales and marketing at the Xerox Corporation. A qualified peer-visitor at the Walter Reed National Army Medical Center in Washington, DC, he offers counseling to veteran amputees.

One of the most sought-after minds in strategic communications, **Rakia Reynolds** (chapter 4) is a thought leader, tastemaker, and branding expert who advises top Fortune 500 companies on creative strategy. Rakia serves as Founder and CEO of public relations agency Skai Blue Media. A non-traditional agency, Skai Blue Media is a proudly eclectic group of storytellers, brand experts, and strategists. Recently, she served as creative director for Philadelphia's bid for Amazon H2Q—which resulted in landing Philly as a top-20 finalist from contending cities across the country.

About the Contributors

Andrew Stine (chapter 21) has been a sixth-grade teacher at Twin Valley Middle School in Elverson, Pennsylvania, for six years. He has his master's degree in educational leadership and has earned an Administrative Certificate. He has taken on many additional responsibilities in his school community and, in 2017, received the Citadel Heart of Learning Award for excellence in education.

Doug Yearley (chapter 1) joined Toll Brothers in 1990 and has held various management positions over the past twenty-eight years. Initially specializing in land acquisitions and project management, Doug learned the home building business from the ground up. Doug was promoted to CEO in June 2010 and contributes to Toll Brothers as a member of the Board of Directors.

www.ingramcontent.com/pod-product-compliance
Lightning Source LLC
Chambersburg PA
CBHW030143240426
43672CB00005B/254